Best,

D0861002

Larry Massie

FROM FRONTIER FOLK TO FACTORY SMOKE:

Michigan's First Century of Historical Fiction

by
Larry Massie

5-16-90

FROM FRONTIER FOLK TO FACTORY SMOKE:

Michigan's First Century of Historical Fiction

Introductions by
Larry Massie
Allegan, Michigan

Copyright 1987
by Larry Massie
and
Avery Color Studios
Au Train, Michigan 49806

Library of Congress Card No. 87-70568
ISBN 0-932212-50-6
First Edition - March 1987
Published by Avery Color Studios

Table of Contents

Introduction   I

Flavius J. Littlejohn
Legends of Michigan and the Old Northwest (1875)   9

James Fenimore Cooper
The Oak Openings; or, The Bee-Hunter (1848)   17

Simon Pokagon
Queen of the Woods (1899)   32

Caroline Kirkland
A New Home—Who'll Follow? (1839)   41

Benjamin F. Taylor
Theophilus Trent: Old Times in the Oak
Openings (1887)   47

Orlando B. Willcox
Walter March; or, Shoepac Recollections (1856)   59

Henry H. Riley
Puddleford and Its People (1854)   71

Jerome James Wood
The Wilderness and the Rose (1890)   80

Eugene Thwing
The Red Keggers (1903)   90

Charles W. Jay
My New Home in Northern Michigan (1874)   102

Stewart Edward White
The Blazed Trail (1902)   108

Harold Titus
"Timber" (1922)   116

James North Wright
Where Copper Was King (1905)   129

Geoffrey Dell Eaton
Backfurrow (1925)   145

Lawrence H. Conrad
Temper (1924)   160

Arnold Mulder
The Sand Doctor (1921)   171

INTRODUCTION

The ranks of veteran volumes stand stiffly at attention. Some gleam resplendent in pristine bindings and gilt edges. Others, dog eared and shabby, bear the battle scars inflicted by many generations of readers. The oldest books, from the 1830's, 40's and 50's, wear blind stamped cloth bindings, simple and austere, like the times. The bright colors and elaborate decoration of late nineteenth century examples mirror Victorian taste in architecture and furniture. Some few from the twentieth century sport gaudy dust jackets. The appearance of still others, rebound in shiny buckram, spines tattooed with call numbers and end papers ignominiously stamped "discard", documents their public library provenance.

A century of Michigan novels, and what stories they hold. Locked within yellowing pages lie thrilling tales about Potawatomi chiefs and pioneer courage, lumberjacks and copper miners, steam locomotives chugging across the peninsulas and the irresistible fury of a Lake Michigan gale, life on the farm and work in automobile plants. The colorful gamut of Michigan's past has been captured by succeeding generations of novelists. Are these novels to be half - forgotten relics of interest only to antiquarians or a vital source for rediscovering and enjoying our state's heritage?

My interest in Michigan fiction originated as a by-product of book collecting. For decades I habituated used book stores, library sales, auctions, estate sales and anywhere else old books might be found. As my goal to develope a comprehensive selection of books dealing with Michigan history broadened to encompass books published within Michigan or written by Michiganians, I began acquiring various works of fiction. Volumes of poetry bearing Michigan imprints sometimes contained information on local history, but the quality of the verse precluded much reading. However, when I sampled novels set in Michigan, I found much to my liking.

Everyone enjoys reading a good story, but I gradually realized that these fictional accounts of Michigan life had value beyond the plot. I found picturesque description and details unavailable in more traditional historical sources. When I researched the authors' lives, I discovered that their novels were often autobiographical accounts. Many writers were, in fact, historical participants who had utilized fiction as a medium to record their experiences.

Caroline Kirkland described her own life on the Michigan frontier during the 1830's in A NEW HOME WHO'LL FOLLOW. Henry H. Riley based PUDDLEFORD AND ITS PEOPLE, first published in 1854, on his experiences in early Constantine. Charles W. Jay paused from his attempt at carving a homestead out of Oceana County wilderness to pen a humorous account of his activities in 1874, MY NEW HOME IN NORTHERN MICHIGAN. James N. Wright drew upon his career of over forty years in the upper peninsula copper mines to create WHERE COPPER WAS KING in 1905.

Some authors like Caroline Kirkland and Charles W. Jay recorded their experiences very soon after they had occured. Others waited many years before reminiscing in a novel. Simon Pokagon wrote his autobiographical account as an old man in 1899. Similarly, Benjamin Taylor's THEOPHILUS TRENT, published in 1882, recounted his adventures as a school teacher on the Michigan frontier of the 1830's.

Authors of substantial literary fame including James Fenimore Cooper, Stewart Edward White, James Oliver Curwood and Ernest Hemingway wrote works set in Michigan. Other less distinguished authors, whose novels never circulated far from their home towns, also contributed prose of significant historical value. Literary historians cite Michigan novels as among the earliest examples of regional fiction, and Caroline Kirkland's writings stand as pioneer examples of realism.

Because the fiction writer's craft requires a well developed descriptive skill, novels often portray historic scenes in a detail lacking in traditional histories. Charles Dickens' colorful novels, for example, have immortalized aspects of 19th century British society. Michigan novelists have preserved Indian lodge tales, lost arts like bee hunting, folk remedies and pioneer recipes. Examples of genuine frontier dialects survive only in certain novels. Fictional word portraits evoke the past in a manner unmatched by historical accounts. Early Michigan society comes to life. We can smell the virgin wilderness, hear the rhythmic chopping of the shanty boys, feel the heat of a roaring forest fire, follow the copper miners into their subterranean world or experience the monotony and depression of life in the automobile factories.

In short, the pages of Michigan novels provide a glimpse into the past, an interesting and effortless manner of learning history. Unfortunately very few older Michigan novels continue to be read. Even specialists in Michigan history are often unaware of their existence. Almost all are out of print, many do not appear regularly on the used book market and erstwhile librarians,, eager to update their holdings, have relegated many a Michigan novel to the dumpster. This volume then, represents my efforts to promote and make available a genre that stands in danger of being lost forever.

I have consulted bibliographies, examined more than one hundred novels set in Michigan and thoroughly read nearly half of that number. I have chosen selections that seem to typify the diversity of literary styles, portray some important element of Michigan's past, and can stand alone without a detailed knowledge of the novel's entire plot. Originally, I decided to include only novels that were published prior to World War II. The later works seemed better known by the reading public and more readily available. Copyright considerations further reduced the field.

This volume is intended to make available some good Michigan writing, literature that should not be forgotten. Maybe the genre itself will also be promoted. Hopefully some readers will be inspired by these excerpts to read the original volumes in their entirety or to seek out other novels not included here. Welcome to the fascinating world of historic Michigan novels.

Larry B. Massie
Allegan, Michigan

LEGENDS OF MICHIGAN
AND THE OLD NORTHWEST

EARLY travelers frequently waxed poetic over Michigan's scenery. Descriptions of virgin forests, parklike oak-openings, stretches of waving prairie grass and uncluttered beaches as far as the eye could see cause modern nature lovers to yearn for the sights and smells of the unspoiled wilderness. The pioneer days are long gone, but fiction can be a time machine to convey us back to a simpler, more natural Michigan.

Once the site of Michigan's largest natural prairie, Prairie Ronde, today farmlands, fertile and level, stretch out on all sides from the village of Schoolcraft in southern Kalamazoo County. Flavius J. Littlejohn takes us back to the Prairie Ronde he first saw in 1836.

Littlejohn was born in Herkimer County, New York in 1804. He graduated from Hamilton College in 1827, became a lawyer in 1830, and set up practice in Little Falls, New York. Seeking to rebuild his poor health, Littlejohn immigrated to Allegan, Michigan in 1836. For several years he served as a surveyor, engineer and geologist. State politics beckoned, and he was elected a representative in 1842, 1843, 1848 and 1855 and a state senator in 1845-46. Littlejohn returned to the practice of law in 1848 and ten years later was elected judge of the Ninth Circuit which comprised 20 counties along the eastern shore of Lake Michigan from Van Buren to Emmet.

Littlejohn's extended travels as a surveyor, geologist and circuit-riding judge brought him into contact with scattered bands of Indians. Over a period of forty years he gathered the legends of lodge tales he heard recited around crackling campfires. In 1875 Littlejohn published in Allegan a collection of these stories, LEGENDS OF MICHIGAN AND THE OLD NORTHWEST. Although written in the typically stilted style of his times Littlejohn's book sold well and soon won a reputation as a legitimate source of Indian lore. The following selection is taken from "The Shawnee and Pottowatomie War: or, the Michigan scouts of 1800-1".

Legends of Michigan

PRAIRIE RONDE, on the southern margin of Kalamazoo county, is not surpassed in picturesque loveliness by any of the numerous prairies in Southwestern Michigan. From different standpoints, the natural eye commands a clear view of much of its undulating surface, and its irregular outline limits. A novel charm is added to its scenic beauty by the fact that, entirely separated from the belt or fringe of growing timber encircling the prairie, an island of thrifty forest trees is snugly nestled down upon the bosom of the prairie. This unusual circumstance, doubtless, suggested its name of "Prairie Ronde," or "Prairie Around." Like other Michigan prairies, this one is circumscribed in extent and boundary so as to be crossed from side to side without exhaustive fatigue. It can be readily scanned by the natural eye, without the wearisome sameness of the almost limitless plains further west.

The soil, a dark brown loam, was in its annual product of indigenous grasses, herbage and flowering plants, richly prolific. As the season advanced toward midsummer, there was, in the normal condition of that prairie, with an unclouded sun, a gorgeousness of coloring—a flashing brightness from an infinity of rainbow hues, alternately blended and shifting from clear light to half hidden blooms, which threw a wierd enchantment over the beholder. Let the reader imagine a fringe of dark green foliage far away, skirting the prairie outline and marking the visual horizon. Then let the eye rest on the quiet, cool shadows beneath the group of those central island trees. Mark how the scattering beams of sunlight come piercing and glinting through the leafy canopy, tracing on that velvet carpet fantastic pictures of quivering brightness. Nestled in the shade of that far-skirting green fringe and of that central canopy alike, numberless feathered songsters, perched on bough and branch, warble forth their gladness in gushing notes of sweetest melody. They could not be silent. They could not repress the joyous upbursting song, when thus brought face to face with ravishing beauty.

But that picture within! Gentle reader, can your live-liest fancy grasp it? The time is, when there are drifting patches of fleecy clouds above, causing swift alterna-tions of sunbeam and shadows to chase each other over the scene below. Listen to the chirping of multitudinous insects, and the hum of countless bees. Raise your eye for a glance out upon the rich mantle spread over that grand level stretch of prairie. You find it dotted and spangled, yea, gemmed all over with single stems, and clusters, and groups of flowering shrubs and plants. Upon them there is an infinity of buds and blooming flowers. They are endless in variety, and tinted with every conceivable shade of hue and color. O! There is a briliancy, a gor-geousness, and a glory in that bewildering bloom, not even surpassed by the vivid colors in the bow of the Crea-tor's promise.

Next please call to your aid another scene, and try another test. Your breath is like the fabled ether of Ely-sium; for the very air is permeated and laden with perfumes and fragrant odors from the exquisite aroma of that wilderness of blooms. Finally, and as the crowning glory, just imagine an outreaching, overspreading at-mosphere all aglow, but without drift or current, yet tremulous and shimmering in its own baptism of golden light.

Gentle reader, we simply desired to lay before you a picture of the Prairie Ronde of seventy years by gone; and even as the writer saw it about forty years ago, when clad in the fresh garniture of its virgin wilderness state, and rivaling in its adornments our ideal creations of an earthly paradise.

At evening twilight of a day in early June of the year 1801, two men rode out from the island of timber we have

11

described, upon the northern trail, urging their hardy animals swiftly across the intervening prairie into the forest beyond. Yet rapid and stealthy as their brief transit was, in that gathering nightfall gloaming, they did not escape observation.

There was at that period a projecting arm or neck of the outlaying forest, northeast of the timber island. It stretched into the prairie to within one hundred rods of the trail along which those horsemen were speeding their way. In the western skirts of this wooded neck, but screened from outward view, two other men had for many days been posted, maintaining a sharp outlook upon the stretch of prairie and the course of the trail north from the timber island.

The men last named were our old acquaintances, Dead Shot and Lynx Eye, now on duty as outlying scouts of Wakazoo, and spies upon the movements of any Shawnees going northward from Three Rivers. From their intimate association for the last two years, they conversed readily in the English language. The native, however, inclined to use the abrupt and abbreviated vernacular of unlettered American border men.

No sooner had the two horsemen vanished from sight in their northerly course, than Lynx Eye, rising from his recumbent posture, said, "Me go see 'em trail. May be me tell who 'em be, and where 'em go." Dead Shot replied, "You are right. Be wary and quick. If you fail now, we will have a closer view of their return."

Lynx Eye crept forward through the underbrush. Then he sank from view, so that the keen eyes behind him could only mark his progress by the gentle waving of the tall grass out on the open prairie. But Dead Shot thus knew that the distance was being successfully traversed.

After the lapse of an hour, the scout on the watch was made aware of the approach of his comrade by a skilful imitation of a whippoorwill's notes. The last twilight was then merging in the darkness of an ordinary starlight night. As those notes were echoed back the native scout appeared, quietly seating himself beside the other. Defering to the well-known reticence of all Indian messengers, Dead Shot allowed a few moments to elapse in silence. Then, facing the other, he put the inquiry: "Well, Lynx Eye, who were they?"

The latter as quietly replied, "Shawnees, Gray Wolf and two braves." Dead Shot hastily rejoined, "How is that? There were but two men passed on the trail. But tell me, who is Gray Wolf, and what have you seen on the trail?"

The dwarf answered: "Me tell Dead Shot all. Gray Wolf is young Shawnee chief, smart to talk, and him grow big on war path. Me see tracks of two braves on trail, no more. Then me go up north to forks. You know, three: one go north to river, one other go more toward big lake. Him go to Horse Shoe Bend, to Wakazoo. The last one points toward sunset, to Paw Paw, where Pokagon stays. At Trail Forks, me see nuther horse track, coming up trail from Paw Paw. Three all take middle trail for Horse Shoe Bend. First them have small talk together, me know, cause me see tracks of horses stepping all round. One rider drop this. Me find him there."

Ceasing to speak the dwarf drew out from beneath his garment, an arrow with a flint head. The shaft, slightly flattened near the fastening, had drawn thereon in blue paint, a rude sketch of a wolf's head. Lynx Eye thereupon resumed his remarks: "Me know this, Gray Wolf use him, cause me hear talk of Wakazoo and Mishawaha. Gray Wolf much want to find Elkhart's daughter. Last year him want Mishawaha for wife. Elkhart say no; cause him want much big chief for her. Gray Wolf no give up. Him send one brave to spy her out at Paw Paw. If no find her, him was to come up to Trail Forks. Gray Wolf meet him with nuther brave. All now gone down to Wakazoo's settlement for sharp look after Mishawaha. Better than heap of scalps, Gray Wolf think, to steal her away from Wakazoo. Him spose Elkhart then give him to him for wife. Lynx Eye has spoken."

"Aye, by my faith," said the pale face, "and shrewdly spoken, too. I believe you have hit the mark. But what are we to do? Shall we follow them up on the trail?" The dwarf answered, "Dead Shot know best 'bout that. In course, if you go, me go too."

"You are always ready to follow my lead. But now I am in doubt, I want Lynx Eye to say what he thinks."

"Me think best way to stay here, watch 'em when come back, fore much long."

"Well, we will stay then, and try for a close look as they

14

return. 'Twill be some hours first, meantime we can go to eat and sleep."

"Lynx Eye thinks the talk is good. Him now much tired, and big hungry."

The colloquy here ended, for the two immediately withdrew further within the timber to a small circular hollow of some depth, but screened around its upper verge by a thickly clustered growth of bushes. Carefully parting these they descended the sloping slide. Uncovering some live coals, they placed thereon a few dry sticks, and soon had a clear blaze, with but little smoke to rise and thus betray their presence. Next they broiled some nice venison steaks, cut from the fresh saddle of a deer, stowed away under some boughs. After eating a hearty meal, and smothering down the fire, they slept soundly, wrapped in their blankets, till early dawn. Making a similar repast for breakfast, they resumed their watch in the forest skirts.

There they remained until towards noon when Dead Shot espied a flock of wild turkies out on the prairie within easy rifle range. Mechanically his rifle came up to his shoulder for a shot, but the hand of Lynx Eye was hastily laid on his ·arm, with the low spoken caution—

"Dead Shot too much forget. Rifle make smoke and big noise. Arrow go still, but him kill all same."

The rifle was instantly lowered, while the dwarf, dropping prone on the ground, crept half the distance toward the flock. Then cautiously lifting his head and shoulders above the grass, the arrow sped on its mission of death. A few minutes later and the native scout was again beside the other, exultingly holding up to view a fine turkey gobbler. Dead Shot, smiling approvingly, dismissed him to the hollow to dress and cook the turkey for their dinner, while he would maintain a careful watch upon the trail.

In due time Lynx Eye returned to their place of outlook, bearing the turkey neatly dressed and nicely cooked. Pointing to it, lying upon a square of bark, with a significant glance and motion towards the knife in the belt of the other, he remarked: "Good time as any, and good place to eat him here, can then watch over trail same time."

The turkey was eaten with a relish that only woodsmen know, and the watch was kept up until the sun was sink-

ing below the western tree tops. Then three persons
appeared in view on the northern trail, two of these
urging their jaded and sweat-covered horses towards the
timber island.

OAK OPENINGS

AN author of national reputation, James Fenimore Cooper, chose the Kalamazoo River region as the setting for a novel published in two volumes in 1848. Cooper was born in Burlington, New Jersey in 1789. His father moved the family to a large tract of land he owned on the frontier, now the site of Cooperstown, New York, in 1790. Cooper spent his youth as a pioneer, attended Yale at the age of thirteen and three years later joined the United States Navy. He began his literary career in 1819 with a story of country life, PRECAUTION, as an experiment to improve on the popular novels of the period. His first work proved unsuccessful, but THE SPY, published in 1821, became a best seller. Two years later, Cooper produced the first of his famous "Leatherstocking series", THE PIONEERS, which was followed by THE LAST OF THE MOHICANS, THE PRAIRIE, etc. By the time of his death in 1851 he had authored over 70 volumes. Many of his later novels, however, did not gain the popularity of his earlier works.

Some of Cooper's relatives pioneered in Kalamazoo County, and in the 1840's Cooper himself invested in land in what is now downtown Kalamazoo and elsewhere in the county. He made several trips to Kalamazoo County in 1847 and 1848 on legal and property related matters, and while there secured the information he incorporated into THE OAK OPENINGS OR THE BEE HUNTER. Local legends claim Cooper to have written the novel in any of three possible locations in Kalamazoo County, but journal entries indicate that he produced OAK OPENINGS at his home in Cooperstown. Controversy *also exists as to the model for the leading character, Buzzing Ben. Local residents believed it to be either Prairie Ronde pioneer Bazil Harrison or Towner Savage of Kalamazoo, a bee hunter by vocation. Other later researchers assert the character to be entirely fictitious. Regardless of the unresolved debate over details, and the fact that literary critics consider OAK OPENINGS to be one of Cooper's lesser works, the novel is well worth reading. Local settings, picturesque descriptions, an interesting plot and information on forgotten arts such as bee hunting, offer an entertaining and informative adventure into Michigan's past.*

The Oak Openings

"How doth the little busy bee
Improve each shining hour,
And gather honey all the day,
From every opening flower."
WATT'S Hymns for Children

WE have heard of those who fancied that they beheld a signal instance of the hand of the Creator in the celebrated cataract of Niagara. Such instances of the power of sensible and near objects to influence certain minds, only prove how much easier it is to impress the imaginations of the dull with images that are novel, than with those that are less apparent, though of infinitely greater magnitude. Thus, it would seem to be strange, indeed, that any human being should find more to wonder at in any of the phenomena of the earth than in the earth itself; or, should specially stand astonished at the might of Him who created the world, when each night brings into view a firmament studded with other worlds, each equally the work of his hands!

Nevertheless, there is (at bottom) a motive for adoration, in the study of the lowest fruits of the wisdom and power of God. The leaf is as much beyond our comprehension of remote causes, as much a subject of intelligent admiration, as the tree which bears it: the single tree confounds our knowledge and researches the same as the entire forest; and though a variety that appears to be endless pervades the world, the same admirable adaptation of means to ends, the same bountiful forethought, and the same benevolent wisdom are to be found in the acorn as in the gnarled branch on which it grew.

The American forest has so often been described as to cause one to hesitate about reviving scenes that may possibly pall, and in retouching pictures that have been so frequently painted as to be familiar to every mind. But God created the woods, and the themes bestowed by his bounty are inexhaustible. Even the ocean, with its boundless waste of water, has been found to be rich in its various beauties and marvels; and he who shall bury himself with us, once more, in the virgin forests of this widespread land, may possibly discover new subjects of admiration, new causes to adore the Being that has brought all into existence, from the universe to its most minute particle.

The precise period of our legend was in the year 1812, and the season of the year the pleasant month of July, which had now drawn near to its close. The sun was already approaching the western limits of a wooded view, when the actors in its opening scene must appear on a stage that is worthy of a more particular description.

The region was, in one sense, wild, though it offered a picture that was not without some of the strongest and most pleasing features of civilization. The country was what is termed "rolling," from some fancied resemblance to the surface of the ocean when it is just undulating with a long "ground-swell." Although wooded, it was not as the American forest is wont to grow, with tall, straight trees towering towards the light, but with intervals between the low oaks that were scattered profusely over the view, and with much of that air of negligence that one is apt to see in grounds where art is made to assume the character of nature. The trees, with very few exceptions, were what is called the "burr-oak," a small variety of a very extensive genus; and the spaces between them, always irregular, and often of singular beauty, have obtained the name of "openings"; the two terms combined giving their appellation to this par-ticular species of native forest, under the name of "Oak Openings."

These woods, so peculiar to certain districts of country, are not altogether without some variety, though possessing a general character of sameness. The trees were of very uniform size, being little taller than pear-trees, which they resemble a good deal in form; and having trunks that rarely attain two feet in diameter. The variety is produced by their distribution. In places they stand with a regularity resembling that of an orchard; then, again, they are more scattered and less formal, while wide breadths of the land are occasionally seen in which they stand in copses, with vacant spaces, that bear no small affinity to artificial lawns, being covered with verdure. The grasses are supposed to be owing to the fires lighted periodically by the Indians in order to clear their hunting-grounds.

Towards one of these grassy glades, which was spread on an almost imperceptible acclivity, and which might have contained some fifty or sixty acres of land, the reader is now requested to turn his eyes. Far in the wilderness as was the spot, four men were there, and two of them had even some of the appliances of civilization about them. The woods around were the then unpeopled forest of Michigan, and the small winding reach of placid water that was just visible in the distance was an elbow of the Kalamazoo, a beautiful little river that flows westward,emptying its tribute into the vast expanse of Lake Michigan. Now, this river has already become known, by its villages and farms, and railroads and mills; but then, not a dwelling of more pretension than the wigwam of the Indian, or an occasional shanty of some white adventurer, had ever been seen on its banks. In that day the whole of that fine peninsula, with the exception of a narrow belt of country along the Detroit River, which was settled by the French as far back as near the close of the seventeenth century, was literally a wilderness. If a white man found his way into it, it was an Indian trader, a hunter, or an adventurer in some other of the pursuits connected with border life and the habits of the savages.

Of this last character were two of the men on the open glade just mentioned, while their companions were of the race of the aborigines. What is much more remarkable, the four were absolutely strangers to each other's faces, having met for the first time in their lives only an hour previously to the commencement of our tale. By saying that they were strangers to each other, we do not mean that the white men were acquaintances, and the Indians strangers, but that neither of the four had ever seen either of the party until they met on that grassy glade, though fame had made them somewhat acquainted through their reputations. At the moment when we desire to present this group to the imagination of the reader, three of its number were grave and silent observers of the movements of the fourth. The fourth individual was of middle size, young, active, exceeding well formed, and with a certain open and frank expression of countenance that rendered him at least well-looking, though slightly marked with the small-pox. His real name was Benjamin Boden, though he was extensively known throughout the northwestern territories by the *sobriquet* of Ben Buzz—extensively as to distances, if not as to people. By the *voyageurs,* and other French of that region, he was almost universally styled *Le Bourdon,* or the "Drone"; not, however, from his idleness or inactivity, but from the circumstance that he was notorious for laying his hands on the products of labor that proceeded from others. In a word, Ben Boden was a "bee-hunter," and as he was one of the first to exercise his craft in that portion of the country, so was he infinitely the most skilful and prosperous. The honey of Le Bourdon was not only thought to be purer and of higher flavor than that of any other trader in the article, but it was much the most abundant. There were a score of respectable families on the two banks of the Detroit who never purchased of any one else, but who patiently waited for the arrival of the capacious bark canoe of Buzz, in the autumn, to lay in their supplies of this savory nutriment for the approaching winter. The whole family of griddle cakes, including those of buckwheat, Indian, rice, and wheaten flour, were more or less dependent on the safe arrival of Le Bourdon for their popularity and welcome. Honey was eaten with all; and *wild* honey had a reputation rightfully or not obtained, that even rendered it more welcome than that which was formed by the labor and art of the domesticated bee.

The dress of Le Bourdon was well adapted to his pursuits and life. He wore a hunting-shirt and trowsers, made of thin stuff, which was dyed green, and trimmed with yellow fringe. This was the ordinary forest attire of the American rifleman; being of a character, as it was thought, to conceal the person in the woods, by blending its hues with those of the forest. On his head Ben wore a skin cap, somewhat smartly made, but without the fur; the weather being warm. His moccasins were a good deal wrought, but seemed to be fading under the exposure of many marches. His arms were excellent; but all his martial accoutrements, even to a keen, long-bladed knife, were suspended from the rammer of his rifle; the weapon itself being allowed to lean, in careless confidence, against the trunk of the nearest oak, as if their master felt there was no immediate use for them.

Not so with the other three. Not only was each man well armed, but each man kept his trusty rifle hugged to his person, in a sort of jealous watchfulness; while the other white man, from time to time, secretly, but with great minuteness, examined the flint and priming of his own piece. This second pale-face was a very different person from him just described. He was still young, tall, sinewy, gaunt, yet springy and strong, stooping and round-shouldered, with a face that carried a very decided top-light in it, like that of the notorious Bardolph. In short, whiskey had dyed the countenance of Gershom Waring with a tell-tale hue, that did not less infallibly betray his destination than his speech denoted his origin, which was clearly from one of the States of New England. But Gershom had been so long at the Northwest as to have lost many of his peculiar habits and opinions, and to have obtained substitutes.

Of the Indians, one, an elderly, wary, experienced warrior, was a Pottawattamie, named Elksfoot, who was well-known at all the trading-houses and "garrisons" of the Northwestern Territory, including Michigan, as low down as Detroit itself. The other redman was a young Chippewa, or O-jeb-way, as the civilized natives of that nation now tell us the word should be spelled. His ordinary appellation among his own people was that of Pigeonswing; a name obtained from the rapidity and length of his flights. This young man, who was scarcely turned of five-and-twenty, had already obtained a high reputation among the numerous tribes of his nation as a messenger or "runner."

Accident had brought these four persons, each and all strangers to one another, in communication in the glade of the Oak Openings, which has already been mentioned, within half an hour of the scene we are about to present to the reader. Although the rencontre had been accompanied by the usual precautions of those who meet in a wilderness, it had been friendly so far; a circumstance that was in some measure owing to the interest they all took in the occupation of the bee-hunter. The three others, indeed, had come in on different trails, and surprised Le Bourdon in the midst of one of the most exciting exhibitions of his art—an exhibition that awoke so much and so common an interest in the spectators as at once to place its continuance for the moment above all other considerations. After brief salutations, and wary examinations of the spot and its tenants, each individual had, in succession, given his grave attention to what was going on, and all had united in begging Ben Buzz to pursue his occupation, without regard to his visitors. The conversation that took place was partly in English, and partly in one of the Indian dialects, which luckily all the parties appeared to understand. As a matter of course, with a sole view to oblige the reader, we shall render what was said, freely, into the vernacular.

"Let's see, let's see, *stranger*," cried Gershom, emphasizing the syllable we have put in italics, as if especially to betray his origin, "what you can do with your tools. I've heer'n tell of such doin's, but never see'd a bee lined in all my life, and have a desp'rate fancy for larnin' of all sorts, from 'rithmetic to preachin'."

"That comes from your Puritan blood," answered Le Bourdon, with a quiet smile, using surprisingly pure English for one in his class of life. "They tell me you Puritans preach by instinct."

"I don't know how that is," answered Gershom, "though I can turn my hand to anything. I heer'n tell, across at Bob Ruly (*Bois Brule*[1]), of sich doin's, and would give a week's keep at Whiskey Centre to know how 't was done."

[1]This unfortunate name, which it may be necessary to tell a portion of our readers means "Burnt Word," seems condemned to all sorts of abuses among the linguists of the West. Among other pronunciations s that of "Bob Ruly"; while an island near Detroit, the proper name of which is "Bois Blanc," is familiarly known to the lake mariners by the name of "Bobolo."

"Whiskey Centre" was a sobriquet bestowed by the fresh-water sailors of that region, and the few other white adventurers of Saxon origin who found their way into that trackless region, firstly on Gershom himself, and secondly on his residence. These names were obtained from the intensity of their respective characters in favor of the beverage named. *L'eau de mort* was the place termed by the *voyageurs,* in a sort of pleasant travesty on the *eau de vis* of their distant, but still well-remembered manufactures on the banks of the Garonne. Ben Boden, however, paid but little attention to the drawling remarks of Gershom Waring. This was not the first time he had heard of "Whiskey Centre," though the first time he had ever seen the man himself. His attention was on his own trade, or present occupation; and when it wandered at all, it was principally bestowed on the Indians; more especially on the runner. Of Elk's foot, or Elksfoot, as we prefer to spell it, he had some knowledge by means of rumor; and the little he knew rendered him somewhat more indifferent to his proceedings than he felt towards those of the Pigeons-wing. Of this young redskin he had never heard; and while he managed to suppress all exhibition of the feeling, a lively curiosity to learn the Chippewa's business was uppermost in his mind. As for Gershom, he had taken *his* measure at a glance, and had instantly set him down to be what in truth he was, a wandering, drinking, reckless adventurer, who had a multitude of vices and . bad qualities, mixed up with a few that, if not absolutely redeeming, served to diminish the disgust in which he might otherwise have been held by all decent people. In the meanwhile, the bee-hunting, in which all the spectators took so much interest, went on. As this is a process with which most of our readers are probably unacquainted, it may be necessary to explain the *modus operandi,* as well as the appliances used.

The tools of Ben Buzz, as Gershom had termed these implements of his trade, were neither very numerous nor very complex. They were all contained in a small, covered wooden pail like those that artisans and laborers are accustomed to carry for the purposes of conveying their food from place to place. Uncovering this, Le Bourdon had brought his implements to view, previously to the moment when he was first seen by the reader. There was a small covered cup of tin; a wooden box; a sort of plate, or platter, made also of wood; and a common tumbler, of a very inferior, greenish glass. In the year 1812 there was not a pane, nor a vessel, of clear, transparent glass made in all America! Now, some of the most beautiful manufactures of that sort known to civilization are abundantly produced among us, in common with a thousand other articles that are used in domestic economy. The tumbler of Ben Buzz, however, was his countryman in more senses than one. It was not only American, but it came from the part of Pennsylvania of which he was himself a native. Blurred, and of a greenish hue, the glass was the best that Pittsburg could then fabricate, and Ben had bought it only the year before, on the very spot where it had been made.

An oak, of more size than usual, had stood a little remote from its fellows, or more within the open ground of the glade than the rest of the "orchard." Lightning had struck this tree that very summer, twisting off its trunk at a height of about four feet from the ground. Several fragments of the body and branches lay near, and on these the spectators now took their seats, watching attentively the movements of the bee-hunter. Of the stump Ben had made a sort of table, first levelling its splinters with an axe, and on it he placed the several implements of his craft, as he had need of each in succession.

The wooden platter was first placed on this rude table. Then Le Bourdon opened his small box, and took out of it a piece of honey-comb that was circular in shape and about an inch and a half in diameter. The little covered tin vessel was next brought into use. Some pure and beautifully clear honey was poured from its spout into the cells of the piece of comb until each of them was about half filled. The tumbler was next taken in hand, carefully wiped, and examined, by holding it up before the eyes of the bee-hunter. Certainly there was little to admire in it, but it was sufficiently transparent to answer his purposes. All he asked was to be able to look through the glass in order to see what was going on in its interior.

Having made these preliminary arrangements, Buzzing Ben—for the *sobriquet* was applied to him in this form quite as often as in the other—next turned his attention to the velvet-like covering of the grassy glade. Fire had run over the whole region late that spring, and the grass was now as fresh and sweet and short as if the place were pastured. The white clover, in particular, abounded, and was then just bursting forth into the blossom. Various other flowers had also appeared, and around them were buzzing thousands of bees. These industrious little animals were hard at work, loading themselves with sweets, little foreseeing the robbery contemplated by the craft of man. As Le Bourdon moved stealthily among the flowers and their humming visitors, the eyes of the two redmen followed his smallest movement, as the cat watches the mouse; but Gershom was less attentive, thinking the whole curious enough, but preferring whiskey to all the honey on earth.

At length Le Bourdon found a bee to his mind, and watching the moment when the animal was sipping sweets from a head of white clover, he cautiously placed his blurred and green-looking tumbler over it, and made it his prisoner. The moment the bee found itself encircled with the glass, it took wing and attempted to rise. This carried it to the upper part of its prison, when Ben carefully introduced the unoccupied hand beneath the glass, and returned to the stump. Here he sat the tumbler down on the platter in a way to bring the honey-comb within its circle.

So much done successfully, and with very little trouble, Buzzing Ben examined his captive for a moment, to make sure that all was right. Then he took off his cap and placed it over tumbler, platter, honey-comb, and bee. He now waited half a minute, when cautiously raising the cap again, it was seen that the bee, the moment a darkness like that of its hive came over it, had lighted on the comb, and commenced filling itself with the honey. When Ben took away the cap altogether, the head, and half of the body of the bee was in one of the cells, its whole attention being bestowed on this unlooked-for hoard of treasure. As this was just what its captor wished, he considered that part of his work accomplished. It now became apparent why a glass was used to take the bee, instead of a vessel of wood or of bark. Transparency

26

was necessary in order to watch the movements of the captive, as darkness was necessary in order to induce it to cease its efforts to escape, and to settle on the comb. As the bee was now intently occupied in filling itself, Buzzing Ben, or Le Bourdon, did not hesitate about removing the glass. He even ventured to look around him, and to make another captive, which he placed over the comb, and managed as he had done with the first. In a minute, the second bee was also buried in a cell, and the glass was again removed. Le Bourdon now signed for his companions to draw near.

"There they are, hard at work with the honey," he said, speaking in English and pointing to the bees. "Little do they think, as they undermine that comb, how near they are to the undermining of their own hive! But so it is with us all! When we think we are in the highest prosperity we may be nearest to a fall, and when we are poorest and humblest, we may be about to be exalted. I often think of these things, out here in the wilderness, when I'm alone, and my thoughts are *actyve*."

Ben used a very pure English, when his condition in life is remembered; but, now and then, he encountered a word which pretty plainly proved he was not exactly a scholar. A false emphasis has sometimes an influence on a man's fortune, when one lives in the world; but it mattered little to one like Buzzing Ben, who seldom saw more than half a dozen human faces in the course of a whole summer's hunting. We remember an Englishman, however, who would never concede talents to Burr, because the latter said, *a l Americaine,* European, instead of European.

"How hive in danger?" demanded Elksfoot, who was very much of a matter-of-fact person. "No see him, no hear him—else get some honey."

"Honey you can have for the asking, for I've plenty of it already in my cabin, though it's somewhat 'arly in the season to begin to work to break in upon the store. In general, the bee-hunters keep back till August, for they think it better to commence work when the creatures,"— this word Ben pronounced as accurately as if brought up at St. James's, making it neither "creatur' " nor "creatoore"—"to commence work when the creatures have had time to fill up, after their winter's feed. But I

27

like the old stock, and, what is more, I feel satisfied this is not to be a common summer, and so I thought I would make an early start."

As Ben said this, he glanced his eyes at Pigeonswing, who returned the look in a way to prove there was already a secret intelligence between them, though neither had ever seen the other an hour before.

"Waal!" exclaimed Gershom, "this is cur'ous, I'll allow *that*; yes, it's cur'ous—but we've got an article at Whiskey Centre that'll put the sweetest honey bee ever suck'd altogether out o' countenance!"

"An article of which you suck your share, friend, I'll answer for it, judging by the sign you carry between the windows of your face," returned Ben, laughing; "but hush, men, hush. That first bee is filled, and begins to think of home. He'll soon be off for *Honey* Centre, and I must keep my eye on him. Now stand a little aside, friends, and give me room for my craft."

The men complied, and Le Bourdon was now all intense attention to his business. The bee first taken had, indeed, filled itself to satiety, and at first seemed to be too heavy to rise on the wing. After a few moments of preparation, however, up it went, circling around the spot, as if uncertain what course to take. The eye of Ben never left it, and when the insect darted off, as it soon did, in an airline, he saw it for fifty yards after the others had lost sight of it. Ben took the range, and was silent fully a minute while he did so.

"That bee may have lighted in the corner of yonder swamp," he said, pointing, as he spoke, to a bit of low land that sustained a growth of much larger trees than those which grew in the "opening," "or it has crossed the point of the wood, and struck across the prairie beyond, and made for a bit of thick forest that is to be found about three miles farther. In the last case, I shall have my trouble for nothing."

"What t'other do?" demanded Elksfoot, with very obvious curiosity.

"Sure enough; the other gentleman must be nearly ready for a start, and we'll see what road *he* travels. 'T is always an assistance to a bee-hunter to get one creature fairly off, as it helps him to line the next with greater sartainty."

Ben *would* say *actyve*, and *sartain*, though he was above saying creatoore, or creatur'. This is the difference between a Pennsylvanian and a Yankee. We shall not stop, however, to note all these little peculiarities in these individuals, but use the proper or the peculiar dialect, as may happen to be most convenient to ourselves.

But there was no time for disquisition, the second bee being now ready for a start. Like his companion, this insect rose and encircled the stump several times ere it darted away towards its hive, in an air-line. So small was the object, and so rapid its movement, that no one but the bee-hunter saw the animal after it had begun its journey in earnest. To *his* disappointment, instead of flying in the same direction as the bee first taken, this little fellow went buzzing off fairly at a right angle! It was consequently clear that there were two hives, and that they lay in very different directions.

Without wasting his time in useless talk, Le Bourdon now caught another bee, which was subjected to the same process as those first taken. When this creature had filled itself, it rose, circled the stump as usual, as if to note the spot for a second visit, and darted away, directly in a line with the bee first taken. Ben noted its flight most accurately, and had his eye on it until it was quite a hundred yards from the stump. This he was enabled to do by means of a quick sight and long practice.

"We'll move our quarters, friends," said Buzzing Ben, good-humoredly, as soon as satisfied with this last observation, and gathering together his traps for a start. "I must angle for that hive, and I fear it will turn out to be across the prairie, and quite beyond my reach for to-day."

The prairie alluded to was one of those small, natural meadows, or pastures, that are to be found in Michigan, and may have contained four or five thousand acres of open land. The heavy timber of the swamp mentioned jutted into it, and the point to be determined was, to ascertain whether the bees had flown *over* these trees, towards which they had certainly gone in an air-line, or whether they had found their hive among them. In order to settle this material question, a new process was necessary.

"I must 'angle' for them chaps," repeated Le Bourdon; "and if you will go with me, strangers, you shall soon see the nicest part of the business of bee-hunting. Many a man who can 'line' a bee can do nothing at an 'angle.' " As this was only gibberish to the listeners, no answer was made, but all prepared to follow Ben, who was soon ready to change his ground. The bee-hunter took his way across the open ground to a point fully a hundred rods distant from his first position, where he found another stump of a fallen tree, which he converted into a stand. The same process was gone through with as before, and Le Bourdon was soon watching two bees that had plunged their heads down into the cells of the comb. Nothing could exceed the gravity and attention of the Indians all this time. They had fully comprehended the business of "lining" the insects towards their hives, but they could not understand the virtue of the "angle." The first bore so strong an affinity to their own pursuit of game as to be very obvious to their senses; but the last included a species of information to which they were total strangers. Nor were they much the wiser after Le Bourbon had taken his "angle"; it requiring a sort of induction to which they were not accustomed, in order to put the several parts of his proceedings together, and to draw the inference. As for Gershom, he affected to be familiar with all that was going on, though he was just as ignorant as the Indians themselves. This little bit of hypocrisy was the homage he paid to his white blood; it being very unseemly, according to his view of the matter, for a pale-face not to know more than a redskin.

The bees were some little time in filling themselves. At length one of them came out of his cell, and was evidently getting ready for his flight. Ben beckoned to the spectators to stand farther back, in order to give him a fair chance, and, just as he had done so, the bee rose. After humming around the stump for an instant, away the insect flew, taking a course almost at right angles to that in which Le Bourdon had expected to see it fly. It required half a minute for him to recollect that this little creature had gone off in a line nearly parallel to that which had been taken by the second of the bees, which he had seen quit his original position. The line led across the neighboring prairie, and any attempt to follow these bees was hopeless.

But the second creature was also soon ready, and when it darted away, Le Bourdon, to his manifest delight, saw that it held its flight towards the point of the swamp, *into* or *over* which two of his first captives had also gone. This settled the doubtful matter. Had the hive of these bees been *beyond* that wood, the angle of intersection would not have been there, but at the hive across the prairie. The reader will understand that creatures which obey an instinct, or such a reason as bees possess, would never make a curvature in their flights without some strong motive for it. Thus, two bees taken from flowers that stood half a mile apart would be certain not to cross each other's tracks, in returning home, until they met at the common hive: and wherever the intersecting angle in their respective flights might be, there would that hive be also. As this repository of sweets was the game Le Bourdon had in view, it is easy to see how much he was pleased when the direction taken by the last of his bees gave him the necessary direction assurance that its home would certainly be found in that very point of dense wood.

QUEEN OF THE WOODS

IF the native Americans portrayed in Littlejohn's and Cooper's work seem lack-lustre and stereotyped try an autobiographical novel written by a full-blooded Michigan Indian Chief. Simon Pokagon was born in 1830 at the old Pokagon Indian village located near Bertrand on the St. Joseph River in southern Berrien County. His father, Leopold Pokagon, a famous Potawatomie chief, had ceeded the land on which Chicago stands to the United States government.

Until he was fourteen, Simon Pokagan could speak no English, but following his education at Notre Dame, Oberlin College and Twinsburg, Ohio he gained the reputation as the "best educated and most distinquished full-blooded Indian in America". Pokagon campaigned many years to get the government to honor the treaty that stipulated payment for the sale of a million acres of land. He visited Presidents Lincoln and Grant, and finally in 1896 the government awared $150,000 to his band.

At the time of the 1893 Columbian Exposition, Pokagon wrote a poem THE RED MAN'S GREETING, a lament for his people's demise. The little volumes were printed on birch bark and circulated at the exposition. He also contributed articles about Indian culture to a variety of magazines during the 1890's. Pokagon wrote the autobiographical novel, QUEEN OF THE WOODS, just prior to his death at his home in Lee Township, Allegan County in 1899. Charles H. Engle of Hartford, Michigan published the volume, and it became a local best seller, running rapidly through three editions. A special feature of Pokagon's style is his use of Potawatomie words and expressions.

O-GI-MAW-KWE MIT-I-GWA-KI

(Queen of the Woods)

ON my return home from Twinsburg, O., where I had attended the white man's school for several years, I had an innate desire to retire into the wild woods, far from the haunts of civilization, and there enjoy myself with bow and arrow, hook and line, as I had done before going to school. Judging from my returning love of the chase, and from various conversations with educated people of the white race, I have come to the conclusion that there is a charm about hunting and fishing, planted deep in the human heart by Nature's own hand, that requires but little cultivation to lead the best educated of even the most civilized races to engage heartily in the sport. Hence I have been forced to the conclusion that when our children are educated, and return from school to live among their own people, unless places can be secured for them away from the influences that cluster about them, the result of their education must necessarily in some cases prove disappointing to those who have labored so ardently in their behalf. In fact I have personal knowledge of a few cases where educated children of our race, instead of influencing their own people to a higher standard of civilization, have themselves fallen back into the ancient customs of their own people. This, however, should in nowise discourage our educators, or be regarded by them as an impeachment of the possibiliities of our children; for I believe with all my heart that if white children were placed under like conditions and circumstances, the result would be similar.

I knew no other language but my mother tongue until past twelve years of age. In those days I took great pleasure in hunting, fishing, and trapping with an old man by the name of Bertrand. There are many white men yet living who were personally acquainted with that remarkable man. He was a person well calculated to please and instruct a boy in his knowledge of the habits of animals, and of places and things with which he was personally acquainted. He was of medium height, uncommonly broad shouldered, and well developed in body and limb. When laughing, or excited in talking, he opened his mouth so wide that his great double teeth could be plainly seen. He always appeared in the best of spirits, having the most hearty laugh of any man I ever knew. As old as I now am, I would walk twenty miles to hear such a laugh. His skin was dark for an Indian, notwithstanding he claimed to be one-quarter French. When speaking of himself, he always talked as if he was a white man. On public occasions among our people, owing to his strength and courage, he was regarded as a sort of police force. I recollect one day during a feast some "auqua" (women) came running to him in great excitement, telling him some half-breeds had brought "awsh-kontay-ne-besh" (firewater) with them, and were giving some to little boys. He started for them on the double-quick, and before they realized what he was doing, he seized all their bottles and broke them against a rock. There were three in the party, and they all rushed for him with sticks and clubs. He knocked each one down in turn with a single blow of his fist. As they lay on the ground, a white man present said, "Bertrand, you struck those Indians awful blows." The old man straightened himself up, saying, "Ae (Yes;) me tells you me did. Au-nish-naw-be-og (Indians) hab no idea how hard a white man can strike." For that timely reproof he was given a place at the head of the feast.

He prided himself in speaking English, which he always tried to do if any were present who he thought understood the language.

Among his white neighbors, he was always referred to as "the 'Injun' who murders the English language." A short time after my return from school I called on the old man. I told him that I had just returned from three years' hard study, and would like to have him take mother and me to some wild retreat where I might spend my vacation in hunting and fishing. He seemed highly pleased with the idea, and told me that he knew of a place up big "Sebe" that could be reached by boat in less than one day's sail, where there was an old abandoned wigwam. It was the wildest place that could be found within fifty miles, and there was an abundance of game and fish. Arrangements were made at once, whereby mother and I were to bring our goods to the river on the following day, where he would meet us with his big dugout canoe. As agreed, we all met on the banks of the beautiful "Sebe", loaded our goods into the boat, and pushed off from shore, he at the paddle and I at the helm, with mother and Maw-kaw, our family dog, as passengers. About noon, as we were quietly making our way up the stream, we caught sight of "mi-tchi-sib-wan" (an osprey) with folded wings plunging headlong with the roar of a rocket into the water a short distance from "o-tchi-man" (our boat), and while yet the water surged and foamed where she went down, she arose to the surface, and tried to rise in air, but could not, floundering about in a zigzag course toward the shore. We gave chase with the boat, and as we overhauled the struggling bird we saw, to our surprise, that she had clutched her claws into the back and near the head of "ogaw" (a pickerel) so large that she could not raise it above the surface of the water, and was trying in vain to loose her hold. The old man seized his dipnet, scooped up both osprey and fish, and dropped them into the bottom of the boat. He then grasped with all his might into the gills of the fish, while I seized the osprey with both hands about the wings. We then pulled the unhappy pair apart,—while the old dog continued to whine as if a tom-tom was being beaten in his ears. "Vell, vell," exclaimed the old man, "I kakkalate dat meby dis chase, and the funny catch, do make you feel gooder than to be at school good many years." He then dropped the fish into the bottom of the boat and asked, "Sime, what one of these two do you feel badest for and villing to let go,—dat bud or de vish?" I replied, "The bird, of course." He then asked "nin-gaw" (my mother) the same question, who replied likewise. He then said, "Dat be right; it's not in uman natre to veel bad for vishes, so we will keep de vish, and eat 'im to-night, and let de bud go." I then asked, "Can you explain why we feel more sorrow for bin-es-si (the bird), when in fact she got fast in trying to kill the innocent gi-go (fish)?"

He replied, "I tink meby I can. You know, Sime, dat de vish hab no love at all; da eat um up one an uder,—eat um their own shilren,—and we like to eat um vish, but no like um osprey." He then grasped hold of the bird's tail-feathers and pulled them out, saying, "Now let 'im go; des quills am good for your cap like um mi-gi-si mig-wan (eagle quills)." The old man now became much excited, and as we rode along, he would point to where he had trapped "jang-we-she" (mink), "wa-jask" (muskrat), and "a-se-pan (coon). At times he would laugh out most heartily in telling how some animals had outwitted him, springing and upsetting his traps; then in telling how he had finally succeeded in catching them, would again laugh more heartily than before.

Just as "gi-siss" (the sun) was going down, we reached our landing-place. The shore on either side was fringed with rushes, flags, and golden-rod, and grasses tall between; and scattered here and there wild roses breathed their rich perfume, scenting the evening air.

Leaving "tchi-man" (the boat), we ascended the banks of the stream, and went some distance round an abrupt headland, beyond which lay "o-ga-be-shi-win aki" (our camping ground). It was indeed a strange, romantic place. A great wigwam there stood. Apparently it had been located so as not to be seen by any that might pass up and down "se-bin" (the stream). It was built of logs of giant size, and, one might well conclude, was intended for wigwam and "wa-ka-i-gan" (fort) as well. The grounds about were carpeted with "mash-kos-su" (grass). The underbrush had been cleared off years before, leaving the towering trees, which hung their archways of green high above the lawn. As we opened the door of the deserted wigwam, it creaked on its hinges like the cry of murder, which "pas-we-we" (echo) repeated in one continuous wailing through "mit-ig" (the woods). Old dog Maw-kaw, startled at the sound, bellowed out a howl-like cry, which, intermixed with the shrieking roar, died away, leaving a strange impress on the soul! Slowly we entered in. Birds flew all about the spacious room, chirping a wild alarm, and brushing our heads with their wings to frighten us away. "O-was-is-swan" (their nests) hung from roof and wall throughout the room. Soon they quieted down, taking to their nests again, but watched us with suspicious eyes. In one corner of the room, was "mi-chi-bo-daw-wan" (a huge fireplace), with chimney built of "mit-i-gons" (sticks) and "wa-bi-gan" (clay); in it, we built a hasty "ish-ko-te" (fire).

Unlike most men of our race, the old man would dress "gi-go" (the fish) and cook it, too. This, with "maw-da-min" (corn cakes) and salt, furnished a splendid meal, of which we ate, thanking the Great Spirit, the cook, and the bird that caught the fish. As night came on, with our blankets wrapped about us, we all lay down to sleep. By the embers' red light, bats were seen flitting about the spacious room, dodging here and there, and then out of sight, while, with a soft, whizzing sound, "ja-gash-an-dawe" (flying squirrels) passed and repasssed above us in curved lines from wall to wall.

It was indeed an ancient, novel place. Long before the break of day, "ak-i-we-si" (the old man) rose and started homeward, as he had promised his family he would be home at noon. I seized my bow and arrows, telling mother I might not be in until after sunrise. "Go on," she said, "only leave Maw-kaw with me." After seeing the old man safely off "pin-dig-ki tchi-man" (in his boat), I carefully climbed to the top of the high headland we had passed around the night before, which like a sentinel, for untold centuries, had guarded the river's valley deep below. I there found an open field, which, from all appearance, had been used during the Indian wars as a lookout for enemies. Here by the faint light of the moon and the glimmering of the stars I dimly surveyed the wild region about me.

It was a beautiful, quiet morning. All nature slept, until the morning feathered bells rang out—"Whip-poor-will! Whip-poor-will! Whip-poor-will!" Slowly, but surely, the curtain of night was lifted from the stage of the woodland theater; above me, one by one the stars hid themselves, the moon grew pale; while all the warblers of the woods opened their matinee, free to all, chanting from unnumbered throats, "Rejoice and praise Him! Rejoice and be glad! Rejoice! Rejoice! Just as the sun tinged the topmost branches of the highland trees, a white fog-cloud appeared above the winding river as far as eye could reach. It looked as though the stream had risen from its ancient bed, and was floating in mid-air. As in wonder and admiration I gazed upon it, a gentle breeze bore it away far beyond the valley from which it arose; and yet it still retained all the curves and angles of the stream until it passed beyond my sight.

While enraptured, there I stood, beholding the beautiful scenery hung by Nature's hand, and listening to the woodland choir, loud the alarm birds (blue jays) screamed out their hawk-like cries. Abruptly the concert closed, and all was still! Looking up, I saw advancing toward me across the open field, a herd of deer, feeding as they came. Quietly stepping behind a bush, I selected the patriarch of the flock, and as he passed broadside before me, in three heart-beats of time, I three successive arrows sent into his side. He ran one breath, and headlong, dying fell. Quickly bleeding and disemboweling him, I carried him across my shoulders down a trail through the woods toward the old wigwam. Coming to "mit-ig" (a fallen tree) of monstrous size, I laid the deer thereon; and while resting there, I heard the sweet voice of my mother, singing in her native tongue,—

"From Greenland's icy mountains,
From India's coral strand,
Where Afric's sunny fountains,
Roll down their golden sand,
From many an ancient river,
From many a palmy plain,
They call us to deliver
Their land from error's chain."

I had heard her sing it many times before, but never did it reach my soul so touchingly as then. Stooping low so as to get a view below the branches of the trees, I could plainly see the old log cabin, and my mother in front of it. I listened until she sang the whole of that beautiful hymn. It so filled my heart with love divine that in my soul I saw Jesus standing with one hand on the sinner's head and the other resting on the throne of the Great Spirit, saying, "Come unto me." After singing each stanza, and sometimes when half finished she would pause and listen, as if she loved to hear the echoing angel of the woods join in the refrain. As she closed the sacred song, I approached cautiously behind her, and threw my burden down. She screamed aloud, and turning quickly around, gazed a moment in silence, then laughed until all the woods replied. She took hold of the arrows, still fast in his side; praised me for my unforgotten skill; would feel his newly grown, soft, and velvet horns, exclaiming, "Kwaw-notch, kwaw-notch maw-mawsh-kay-she (beautiful, beautiful deer)! How could you have o-daw (the heart) to take nin bim-a-dis-win (his life)?" After breakfast she skinned the deer, and prepared the meat for jerked venison for future use, according to our ancient custom.

While living in that secluded place, I felt a freedom and independence unknown to civilization. There, undisturbed, I could hunt and fish, contemplating the romantic beauties and wonderful grandeur of the forests about me. While in communion with the Great Spirit, I could feel, as my fathers had before me, that I was chief of all I surveyed.

A NEW HOME - WHO'LL FOLLOW

THE opening of the Erie Canal in 1825 and the introduction of passenger ships on Lake Erie made immigration to Michigan much more appealing. During the late 1820's and 1830's pioneers flooded into Detroit and fanned out across southern Michigan establishing homesteads and town sites. The William Kirkland family journeyed from western New York state to Detroit in 1835. Kirkland had been offered the job of principal of the Detroit Female Seminary. His 35 year old wife, Caroline, cultured and one of the most highly educated women in America, mothered their four young children and taught in the seminary.

Kirkland began buying land in Livingston County, sixty miles northwest of Detroit, and by the end of 1836 he had acquired 800 acres. He resigned his position to lay out a settlement, the town of Pinckney. In the autumn of 1837, the Kirklands moved to their holdings on the frontier. Caroline described her experiences on the wilderness road in the selection that follows.

In 1839 Caroline Kirkland published A NEW HOME - WHO'LL FOLLOW, a novel based upon her frontier experiences. Pinckney became Montacute, and various local characters appeared in thinly disguised roles. James Fenimore Cooper had described the frontier in a romantic manner, but Caroline Kirkland employed a satirical style to provide the first realistic description of the midwest.

Kirkland's neighbors in Pinckney grew furious over her apparently condescending parody. In 1843 the family returned to New York, and Caroline spent the remainder of her life engaged in literary pursuits and teaching. She wrote two more books about her Michigan experiences, edited THE UNION MAGAZINE and traveled extensively abroad. She became one of the leading female literary figures of her time. When she died in 1864, her pallbearers included William Cullen Bryant and Nathaniel Willis. Caroline Kirkland's A NEW HOME is among the first midwestern novels and remains one of the best satirical descriptions of life on the Michigan frontier.

A New Home - Who'll Follow

Moving Day On The Wilderness Road

AT length came the joyful news that our moveables had
arrived in port; and provision was at once made for their
transportation to the banks of the Turnip. But many and
dire were the vexatious delays, thrust by the cruel Fates
between us and the accomplishment of our plan; and it
was not till after the lapse of several days that the most
needful articles were selected and bestowed in a large
waggon which was to pioneer the grand body. In this
waggon had been reserved a seat for myself, since I had
far too great an affection for my chairs and tables, to omit
being present at their debarcation at Montacute, in order
to ensure their undisturbed possession of the usual com-
plement of legs. And there were the children to be packed
this time,—little roley-poley things, whom it would have
been in vain to have marked—"this side up," like the rest
of the baggage.

A convenient space must be contrived for my plants
among which were two or three tall geraniums and an
enormous Calla Ethiopica. Then D'Orsay must be ac-
commodated, of course; and, to crown all, a large basket
of live fowls; for we had been told that there was none to
be purchased in the vicinity of Montacute. Besides these,
there were all our travelling trunks; and an enormous
square box crammed with articles which we then in our
greenness considered indispensable. We have since
learned better.

After this enumeration, which yet is only partial, it will
not seem strange that the guide and director of our omni-
bus was to ride "on horseback after we." He acted as a
sort of adjutant—galloping forward to spy out the way,
or provide accommodations for the troop—pacing close
to the wheels to modify our arrangements, to console one
of the imps who had bumped its pate, or to give D'Orsay a
gentle hint with the riding-whip when he made demon-
strations of mutiny—and occasionally falling behind to
pick up a stray handkerchief or parasol.

The roads near Detroit were inexpressibly bad. Many
were the chances against our toppling load's preserving
its equilibrium. To our inexperience the risks seemed
nothing less than tremendous—but the driver so often re-

iterated, "that a'n't nothin'," in reply to our despairing exclamations, and what was better, so constantly proved his words by passing the most frightful inequalities (Michiganice' "sidlings") in safety, that we soon became more confident, and ventured to think of something else beside the ruts and mud-holes.

Our stopping-places after the first day were of the ordinary new country class—the very coarsest accommodations by night and by day, and all at the dearest rate. When everybody is buying land and scarce anybody cultivating it, one must not expect to find living either good or cheap: but, I confess, I was surprised at the dearth of comforts which we observed everywhere. Neither milk, eggs, nor vegetables were to be had, and those who could not live on hard salt ham, stewed dried apples, and bread raised with "salt risin'," would necessarily run some risk of starvation.

One word as to this and similar modes of making bread, so much practised throughout this country. It is my opinion that the sin of bewitching snow-white flour by means of either of those abominations, "salt risin'," "milk emptin's," "bran 'east," or any of their odious compounds, ought to be classed with the turning of grain into whiskey, and both made indictable offences. To those who know of no other means of producing the requisite sponginess in bread than the wholesome hop-yeast of the brewer, I may be allowed to explain the mode to which I have alluded with such hearty reprobation. Here follows the recipe:

To make milk emptin's. Take quantum suf. of good sweet milk—add a teaspoon full of salt, and some water, and set the mixture in a warm place till it ferments, then mix your bread with it; and if you are lucky enough to catch it just in the right moment before the fermentation reaches the putrescent stage, you may make tolerably good rolls, but if you are five minutes too late, you will have to open your doors and windows while your bread is baking.—Verbum sap.

"Salt risin'" is made with water slightly salted and fermented like the other; and becomes putrid rather sooner; and "bran 'east" is on the same plan. The consequences of letting these mixtures stand too long will become known to those whom it may concern, when they shall travel through the remoter parts of Michigan; so I shall not dwell upon them here—but I offer my counsel to such of my friends as may be removing westward, to bring with them some form of portable yeast (the old-fashioned dried cakes which mothers and aunts can furnish, are as good as any)—and also full instructions for perpetrating the same; and to plant hops as soon as they get a corner to plant them in. "And may they better reck the rede, Than ever did th' adviser."

The last two days of our slow journey were agreeably diversified with sudden and heavy showers, and intervals of overpowering sunshine. The weather had all the changefulness of April, with the torrid heat of July. Scarcely would we find shelter from the rain which had drenched us completely—when the sunshine would tempt us forth; and by the time all the outward gear was dried, and matters in readiness for a continuation of our progress, another threatening cloud would drive us back, though it never really rained til we started.

We had taken a newly opened and somewhat lonely route this time, in deference to the opinion of those who ought to have known better, that this road from having been less travelled would not be quite *so deep* as the other. As we went farther into the wilderness the difficulties increased. The road had been but little "worked," (the expression in such cases) and in some parts was almost in a state of nature. Where it wound round the edge of a marsh, where in future times there will be a bridge or drain, the wheels on one side would be on the dry ground while the others were sinking in the long wet grass of the marsh—and in such places it was impossible to discern inequalities which yet might overturn us in an instant. In one case of this sort we were obliged to dismount the "live lumber"—as the man who helped us through phrased it, and let the loaded waggon pass on, while we followed in an empty one which was fortunately at hand—and it was, in my eyes, little short of a miracle that our skilful friend succeeded in piloting safely the top-heavy thing which seemed thrown completely off its centre half a dozen times.

At length we came to a dead stand. Our driver had received special cautions as to a certain *mash* that "lay between us and our home"—to "keep to the right"—to "follow the travel" to a particular point, and then "turn up stream:" but whether the very minuteness and reiteration of the directions had puzzled him, as is often the case, or whether his good genius had for once forsaken him, I know not. We had passed the deep centre of the miry slough, when by some unlucky hair's-breadth swerving, in went our best horse—our sorrel—our "Prince,"—the "off haus," whose value had been speered three several times since we left Detroit, with magnificent offers of a "swop!" The noble fellow, unlike the tame beasties that are used to such occurrences, shewed his good blood by kicking and plunging, which only made his case more desperate. A few moments more would have left us with a "single team," when his master succeeded in cutting the traces with his penknife. Once freed, Prince soon made his way out of the bog-hole and pranced off, far up the green swelling hill which lay before us—out of sight in an instant—and there we sat in the marsh.

There is but one resource in such cases. You must mount your remaining horse if you have one, and ride on till you find a farmer and one, two, or three pairs of oxen—and all this accomplished, you may generally hope for a release in time.

The interval seemed a *leetle* tedious, I confess. To sit for three mortal hours in an open waggon, under a hot sun, in the midst of a swamp, is not pleasant. The expanse of inky mud which spread around us, was hopeless, as to any attempt at getting ashore. I crept cautiously down the tongue, and tried one or two of the tempting green tufts, which looked as if they *might* afford foothold; but alas! they sank under the slightest pressure. So I was fain to regain my low chair, with its abundant cushions, and lose myself in a book. The children thought it fine fun for a little while, but then they began to want a drink. I never knew children who did not, when there was no water to be had.

There ran through the very midst of all this black pudding, as clear a stream as ever rippled, and the waggon stood almost in it!—but how to get at it? The basket which had contained, when we left the city, a store of cakes and oranges, which the children thought inexhaustible, held now, nothing but the napkins, which had enveloped those departed joys, and those napkins, suspended corner-wise, and soaked long and often in the crystal water, served for business and pleasure, till Papa came back.

They're coming! They're coming!" was the cry, and with the word, over went Miss Alice, who had been reaching as far as she could, trying how large a proportion of her napkin she could let float on the water.

Oh, the shrieks and the exclamations! how hard Papa rode, and how hard Mamma scolded! but the little witch got no harm beyond a thorough wetting, and a few streaks of black mud, and felt herself a heroine for the rest of the day.

THEOPHILUS TRENT

MANY Michigan pioneer families emigrated from New York state. They brought a strong tradition of education. The establishment of a school was among the first activities in a pioneer community. Local boards hired school teachers as cheaply as possible, but offered free room and board as a fringe benefit. Usually a teacher boarded around the community, spending a few days with each family in the district. Benjamin Taylor portrayed the experiences of a young teacher as he arrived to board at a frontier log cabin. The time is the 1830's, and the area is the region just west of Monroe.

Benjamin Franklin Taylor, poet, journalist and lecturer, was born in Lowville, New York in 1819. Following graduation from Hamilton Literary and Theological Institute, he pioneered for three years in Michigan. But the severe life proved too much for him, and he returned to New York State. Taylor became literary editor of the Chicago DAILY TRIBUNE in 1845 and during the Civil War won a national following as a result of his vivid battle reports. After the war, he began a career as a freelance writer and lecturer.

Taylor's poetry also won him a national reputation. His several volumes about rural and pioneer themes received praise from Whittier and other leading poets. In 1872 he published a collection of Civil War stories and during the 1870's brought out three additional travel books. Just prior to Taylor's death in 1887, he returned to memories of his youth for a semi-autobiographical novel about his experience on the Michigan frontier. THEOPHILUS TRENT: OLD TIMES IN THE OAK

OPENINGS contains vivid pictures of Michigan pioneer life.

Theophilus Trent

Matilda Ann and Jerusha. —supper, music, and dancing.—hunting stories. —retiring under difficulties.

THE young man wished to wash. *"Jerush! Jerush!"*— two inflections and one emphasis— screamed the mother.

"Marm?" burst in at the door, and the speaker after it.

"You rense the skillet,—no, the spider, skillet's hed inyuns in 't, the spider nothing' but taters, —the Kunnel wants ter wash."

The girl seized the spider much as if she had a runaway kitten by the tail, and whisked it away from a gossip with a poor old bake-kettle, a few dead coals and ashes scattered upon its thick-skulled cover, brought the water and a little gourd of soft-soap, apologetically thus:—

"Cake-soap's gone—smelt good, and Matilda Ann she used the last on her hair when she went ter the shows with Bill Pollock."

"You keep still," exclaimed Matilda Ann, catching the last word "Bits of girls like you should be seen, not hearn."

"You're allus tellin' 'bout being' seventeen. It was nothing but 'n accident; Maw says so. It might a ben me jes as well."

"Now you have made a show o' yerself, yer'd better bring the Kunnel a tow'l." This with considerable dignity.

"I'll make 'nother show," retorted Jerusha, who was just at "the hateful age," and in a provoking sing-song, "I k'n do what *you* can't, anyway;" and she whirled about like a top, until her scanty skirt balooned, and down she squatted,—a big, round calico cheese with the girl's saucy head on the top of it. The towel came apologetically also: "Hain't washed in two week; poundin'-barr'l tumbled to bits in the hot sun, and Paw took the pounder to drive stakes, and the hogs tore up 't other tow'l. Mebby you k'n find a gray spot, and that 'll be clean." As Jerusha presented her shoulder-blades, Theophilus wriggled one hand, then the other, in the pocket with his handkerchief.

"Drat the cat!" sounded Maw's voice from the lean-to. "Matilda Ann, how *did* the cat git inter the flour barr'l?" Then there was a scraping of the sort that sets the children's teeth on edge, and the hospitable woman came in with quite a saucerful of flour, and said genially, "I kin make you a cake, Kunnel, arter all." Theophilus smiled as infants do when fanciful mothers say they hear an angel whisper,—his stomach turned over like a tired man in his sleep,—but he smiled pitifully.

"Go to the stub, Matilda Ann, and bring the pork, an' be sure you button the stub door. I see yesterday that it wabbled."

Theophilus must learn before he died what "the stub" was; and so he asked Matilda Ann, who told him, substantially, that it was a section of a great hollow whitewood tree, set upright, roofed with a broad board, a door cut out of the side, and re-attached with a couple of old boot-strap hinges and a button, wherein, upon shelves sustained by wooden pins, articles of food were stored. A companion tower stood on the other side of the cabin for a smoke-house.

The mother dusted out the spider with her elbow, greased it with a little flap of pork, put in the dough, slashed it across with a knife, gave it a compensation pat with her hand, and careened the utensil propped up with a stone before the splendid fire. The baking cake and the steeping sassafras— though Theophilus had never used the latter as a beverage but always as a *browse*—gave forth a pleasant smell, not to mention certain small slices of pork spluttering in a kettle. Theophilus must be pardoned, for he was as hollow as the long-handled gourd hanging by the brown water-pail.

"Jerush, go to the stub and git the honey, and don't wax it. I 'most forgot your Paw cut a bee-tree last week."

"Hitch right up, Kunnel, the table's sot." Theophilus sat in solitary state, the conversation lulled, every eye was upon him but the father's who was making goose-yokes and a figure-four trap. The mother rocked in the chair with the swinging tail and squealing mice, and watched him. Matilda Ann leaned lazily against the jamb, the toes of one bare foot resting on the instep of the other, and watched him. The hounds sat up, one each side of his stool, swallowed in concert with him, followed the destination of every morsel with their great melancholy eyes, and watched him. Foxhounds always look as if they could shed tears if they felt like it. As for Jerusha, she sat upright as a tenpin on the other side of the table, and watched him. Theophilus gave her one of his pedagogic annihilation looks, but she only giggled. She did not know enough to be awed.

"Jerusha, behave, or I'll send you to bed."

"Maw, I ain't doin' nothin' but seein' the Kunnel eat." Apart from this episode, it was a silent ceremonial. Theophilus left a bit of the cake and a finger's width of pork "for manners." Jerusha swept the deck and the supper was a wreck.

The young man found himself in the chimney-corner performing a very childish trick, Jerusha being sole spectator. Taking the great awkward tongs, he laid the tip of a wet finger upon the leg that would lift by the leverage of the handle, and then turning the tongs adroitly, Jerusha exercised her magnetic power upon the leg that *would n't* lift; and, if the girl ever thought of him again, it was as the wonderful schoolmaster who could make the tongs' legs follow his finger "jes ez he wuz a-min' ter."

Tongs were abandoned, tongues were going, and girl-ish laughter lightly rippled the surface of general conversation. Theophilus was patting a dog and trying to locate his own bedroom, when the trap-maker said, "Kunnel, it spiles huntin' dogs to *much* 'em;" and the hearer booked the word for subsequent examination. Paw told bear stories and Maw followed with witch stories; upon which Jerusha dragged her stool as near the schoolmaster as she could get it, and her mother said, "Paw'll fix a goose-yoke an' make you tote it, ef you don't quit bein' so skeery like."

"You never ketched turkeys, I s'pose, Kunnel." Theophilus assured him he had little acquaintance with them except on a plate. "Well, them fowl's the biggest fools on airth. You build a rail-pen kivered over the top with rails too, an' leave a little place in the fence like an oversized cat-hole, big enough for a turkey to go through with his head down. Then lay a trail o- corn from 'way outside through the gap inter the pen, and them creeters jes nat'rally go peckin' along spang inter the trap. You're a-watchin' way off, but you need n't run to shet 'em in, fur don't you b'lieve they'll run roun' and roun' the pen an' never think o' bobbin' thar pates at that hole to git out? I

50

never could sense the meanin' on 't, but I reck'n thar's a kind o' a sarment in 't better 'n a slazy preacher ken preach. Things is most dangersome wen folks hold thar heads highest; let 'em watch thar *feet*, an' they'll go a heap safter."

So from one thing to another the talk flitted. Then the girls popped old corn in the spider, and when the great white flakes snowed over the floor, girls and hounds all scrambled together. Then there was a lull, except an occasional small musket-shot from the fireplace, for there was no clock to tick off the silence, until the mother broke out in a softly way, singing to herself. Her voice, once a sweet, girlish tone, was faded like her dress, and a little sharpened with much worry and some scolding. It was the "Babes in the Woods," and in crooning eleven stanzas she sang the tune eleven times. It would have grown familiar even to a strange ear, but it was one of Theophilus's earliest recollections. He had shed tears for those hapless babes "a-wanderin' up and down;" he had meditated signal punishment upon the cruel uncle; he had seen "Old Sickles' Wax Figures," and heard the chirp of robin redbreast that "kivered them with leaves," as the old lady rendered it, and he told her.

How she brightened, lifting both hands in her pleased surprise! "An' so you seen them blessed poppets! I've hearn on 'em, an' ef thar's one thing I'd like to do more 'n another afore I die, it's to see them poppets," —how cheap human happiness may be sometimes! —and she resumed her crooning with considerably more animation, when a rasping, reedy sound, like the squawk of a duck, burst from the lean-to, confounded the vocalist, and she exclaimed, "Jerush, come out o' thar!" and Jerush appeared, the family comb in her hand, and a strip of paper drawn across the teeth. Her mother was bound to finish the ballad, when the father snuffed out loftily, "Thet's chicking fee," and snuffed the singer out also. "S'pose I take down the old fiddle an' give you a tune. Play, Kunnel?" He disclaimed the accomplishment.

"P'r'aps you play keards, but thar ain't a full deck in the shanty." Theophilus Trent, A.B., was as delighted as the girls at the prospect of a tune, but even in the momentary excitement an uncomfortable doubt as to his bedroom intruded, accompanied by a regretful wonder whether anybody in the whole world remembered him that night. The last was idle, if not wicked; for did not his mother sit in the far East that minute, with her heart in the West? After much throttling and twanging of the fiddle Paw struck up "Roy's Wife" and no one stirred a foot; but when he dashed off in "Money Musk," the stools were kicked aside, the dogs ran under the table, and mother and daughters went whirling like the colored glass fragments in a kaleidoscope, —Matilda Ann with much natural grace, Jerusha with much lawless freedom, the mother retracing, and not so awkwardly, the steps of her vanished youth.

The tall father stood in a corner, eyes closed, head thrown back and to one side, the heel of the fiddle hugged under his chin, and the bow as lively as a rapier in a French duel; while the rest of the family flung their feet about as if perpetually kicking off loose shoes and caring little about ever finding them again, while the measured barefoot thump sounded like a dance of the churn-dashers. Waltzes as old as the first fiddle followed; then a solo jig by Matilda Ann concluded the saltatory entertainment.

As for Theophilus, sitting in a corner, a fiddle-string ran direct from his head to his toes, and they kept time to the music. He had never danced, —at least not much, and then under his father's immediate supervision, the bow being applied to the dancer and not to the fiddle.

Then the father played "Old Rosin the Beau;" and as the last not of "The Arkansas Traveller" was pulled off the strings, he said, "Jerusha, bring the jug." She produced the clay-colored crockery with its corn-cob cork and a nicked yellow-ware teacup, and he passed them about. All declined but Jerusha, who inclined, if she could have it "sweetled," but she couldn't; and he, swinging up the jug in a back-handed way, and with "Here's luck to yer, Kunnel! and —" finished the sentence with two gurgles and a smack. This reprehensible feat accomplished, he took a corn-cob pipe from his hatband, a leaf of tobacco from a bunch hanging on the wall, ground it in the hollow of one hand with the knuckles of the other, crowded it into the pipe-bowl, crowned it with a live coal, drew up a stool by the hearth, began to pull, and clouds of rank smoke rolled round his head like the coming up of a storm.

Then between whiffs he spoke: "I'm minded ter tell ye, Kunnel, a beaver story thet's hard to beat and sure as shootin'. Tew year ago me 'n another feller trapsed up North fur big game (*puff*) sich as b'ar, deer, and ef so be a painter or two, but they ain't plenty. Wall, we wuz trudgin' along one day (*whiff*), our kits gittin' purty heavy, when we come ter a beaver-dam and the cutest kind o' a pond, but thar warn't stick or stock in sight, an' never hed ben (*puff*), fit ter work inter a dam. It tuk us back, an' our packs let up so we kud n't scacely feel 'em. Whar did thet tim'er come from them beaver used? So we (*whiff*)splored roun' an' went mor'n harf a mild 'long a little ditch thet wuz never dug with no shovel, an' we follered an' follered, ontil we struck a clearin' bigger 'n a couple of door-yards, whar staddles and saplin's an' purty sizable trees hed ben cut. Them stumps (*pipe out*) stood thick as hatchel teeth. We zamined the cuts. No tomahawks done it, ner pig-stickers, ner axes; it wuz jest teeth, and beaver teeth too.

"You see, them beavers foun' a dam-site an- no tim'er, tim'er an' no dam-site. How to git them tew e'modities tergether! But they wuz ekol to 't. They kud n't tug thet tim'er, but mebby they kud *float* it, an' they did. Lookin' over the lay o' the land ez we hed, they foun' thet ef they shud scratch out a kind o' canawl an' let in the water, they could snake thar raw mater'al to whar 't wuz wanted. They scratched, and they did. The dam hed n't ben built more 'n six mon's; an' me an' my mate got down on our marrerbones an' s'arched tell we foun' the hard groun', all scratched whar they'd dragged them trees, —an' a sight of 'em thar wuz, —yis, jest ez plain ez Ingen trails in peace-times. We stud, me an' him, an' looked at each other like two ijits, an' never opened our dinner-traps; an' we guv it up. an' it *keeps* guv'n up.

"Thet night 't war full moon, an' we crep' out to see the beaver. They wuz makin' some repa'rs, an' I hed a right smart chance ter draw a bead on a beaver; but I kud n't. Kud you? It warn't no 'buck fever,' sich as green hunters hev when they sight thar fust deer an' shake so they kud n't hit a meetin-house at ten rod; it's a specie of narvous ager thet ketches 'em. I felt 't would be a kind o' murder to kill a beaver, an' I felt 'nough sight more like taking off my old cap to 'em than shootin'."

He knocked the ashes out of the pipe on his thumbnail and went out. The mother picked things up a little, chucked the rag-bag under a bed, and swept the hearth.

"Wash you feet off, gals."

One got the skillet, the other a kettle, and disappeared; each returning in five minutes with a pair of clean brown feet, shapely as a statue's by a great sculptor, and stood on the hearth, turning those feet, top, sole and heel, and drying them in the firelight. Fire was made before looms.

The old man opened the door to let himself in, and his mouth to let a yawn out at the same instant, and said, "Hustle, gals; it's goin' on ten, an' the stars are shinin' all to oncet, ez Methodies sing at camp-meetin'."

"How did he know the time?" thought the young man, as, drawing his watch, it showed fifteen minutes to ten. He never wasted his time trying to evolve anything from his "inner consciousness," as a tribe of fresh thinkers is given to saying. That starting the mental mill to grind a grist that was never put into the hopper is very fascinating to aesthetic, metaphysical, be-spectacled millers. But poor Theophilus had no other way of finding out how that man knew the time of night, and so he asked.

"W'y, by the shiftin' o' the stars, —some thet's risin' an' some thet's most sot. They are sorter boss fellers; but the rest, the hull bilin' of 'em, do nothin' but wink. I know my stars —*clock* stars I call 'em —by sight, but not by name; but what's the odds? *You* know 'em all, I s'pose."

"Here is this ignorant man," mused Theophilus, "and he has learned to read after his fashion the dial of the sky; and its untarnished lettering is more significant to him than the characters on the face of a kitchen clock. He has not filled the heavens with fanciful mythological shapes. He knows nothing about the the Great Bear, but the 'Dipper' he knows, and the 'P'inters' he knows; but Marak and Dubhe are Greek to him. He can walk in the wilderness, of a clear night, and not be lost. He is astronomer enough for his own poor personal needs."

The moment had come. "Thar's the spar' bed, Kunnel," pointing to one particularly fat,—with straw,—and draped in a red and yellow quilt; "you k'n bunk when you're a-min'ter." The speaker shook himself out of his roomy boots. The mother tucked her head into an unbordered nightcap of neutral tint, set so close about the face that it seemed escaping from a pudding-bag. The father cast off his one suspender. The mother pulled a long brass pin, apparently out of the back of her neck; but really it was to the pillowcase of a dress what the king-bolt is to a wagon,—pull it out, and down comes the vehicle. The girls stood on the hearth, changed feet, and stared. Theophilus watched every move with anxious observation.

He hoped the old man would cover the fire, or the chimney tumble in and extinguish it. But to his confusion, the man, muttering, "Ef I hain't forgot the wood!" pattered out, brought in an armful of limbs and sticks dry as the young man's mouth, tumbled them on to the fire, and trailing one leg of his pantaloons across the floor after him, tumbled himself into bed, and the mother crept after. "Two went to bed, and then there were three."

The hearth was a flare of light, and not a shadow anywhere save in the young man's thought. There the girls stood, changed feet, and watched him. He wondered if it would be a greater loss to the family should the cabin catch fire and burn down right there, than it would be a comfort to him in not having to go to bed as if in a public square in the daytime. He deliberately drew off one boot, then the other; his cravat followed his coat. Then he sat down and wished he was lost in the woods.

Quick-witted Jerusha snickered, indulged in a little pirouette on one foot, comprehended the situation, enjoyed it, and sat down also. Matilda Ann posed with one shoulder against the jamb and looked conscious but contented. A snort by way of overture, and a medley of quarrelsome snores snarled and growled from the occupied bed. This created a diversion, and the girls laughed like a chime of merry bells.

If he could only shake himself, be disrobed and between sheets in a second, as those girls could! The desperate moment had come. He loosened a string or two, freed a button or two, gathered the garment up as if he had himself safe in a bag, so that he could shell himself as a thumb-nail can empty a pea-pod, abruptly exclaimed, "Miss Matilda, don't I hear something in the lean-to?" and to Jerusha, "A drink of water, please," and blindly plunged for the "spar' bed." Matilda was rattling among the pots and the pans, Theophilus was just ready to swirl the yellow "drapery of his couch about him," when something touched his ear. Turning a startled eye, he caught sight of a huge weapon like an old-style Sioux war-club. There stood Jerusha, extending a long-handled gourd of water, with which, in her roguish haste to catch him before he escaped to sleep, she liberally drenched him. Theophilus began to say something in a sputtering way, but she was camped on a stool before the fire, shaking as with an ague. It might have been the play of the fitful light upon her person, or it might have been a convulsion of repressed laughter. Theophilus had misgivings, but he slept as only youth and health can sleep.

The instant before he dropped into oblivion, he vigorously determined to be up and dressed and serene before an eye belonging to either of his next neighbors flew open. The dumb and sightless hours went by, and he woke in a fright lest he had out-slept the night. A great glare did indeed fill the cabin, but it was the newly-made fire of early morning, and the old man, the builder, sat smoking and nodding beside it. Theophilus stole a look at his nearest neighbors,—so near that he might have pulled Jerusha's ear. Two tumbled heads of hair lay upon the lean pillows, one bare arm showing white on the sad-colored quilt. By a merciful dispensation both faces were toward the wall and both girls asleep. The teacher slipped cautiously out of bed, and no sword was ever returned to its scabbard with more military promptness than were those lean legs encased in the pantaloons. The rest was the work of a minute, and he was ready for the innocent enemy; but none too soon.

"Gals, rout out!" growled the father. The heads turned inland, and each owner rose upon a naked elbow and surveyed the situation. Theophilus would have fled ignobly out of doors, but for the fear he might be pelted with derisive giggles. He thought of the Sphinx, and tried to decoy a far-away look into his eyes as if beholding distant ages, and be as nearly like that solemn stone presence as possible. Two hands pulled two frocks lying upon the bed toward two chins, four hands drew two skirts over two heads, and the twain, giving little tugs here and little kicks there, as if dressing their plumage, sat upright and clothed; a few more downward kicks under the bed-covering, swung themselves sidewise one after the other, and there were four feet in a row. Finally, giving themselves a little shake, they stood upon the floor dressed *cap-a-pie,* even as Minerva sprang from the brain of Jupiter. Jerusha made a little claw of each hand and combed her tangled tresses. Matilda Ann smoothed her hair with her open palms, and, the toilet made, the daughters of the household were abroad.

Theophilus declared his intention to resume the journey at once, giving several reasons, but omitting the only one that really influenced his decision. Is not that the way of the most of us, and is it honest, or only diplomatic? He firmly withstood the general protest. Even the dog wagged his tail of invitation. The East was red with the new day, a tavern only eight miles distant, he wanted—indeed, he wanted many things but the principal one was to get away. Yes, he must go.

" 'T'l be a good spell, Kunnel, afore you git breakfas'. They'll treat you better'n we ken at the tavern, though the woman's the man o'the house; but the gals'll git you a snack right now." "What of?" thought Theophilus. Yet he thankfully declined it all.

He had measured his host, and made quite sure a proffer of money, much as he seemed to need it, would "rile" him, as he would express it; so the traveller heartily thanked, what visiting ministers used to pray for, "the united head of his family," and then he gave each of the girls—what was very rare in those regions of monetary rags—a silver coin of generous diameter,—there went two of his three pocket-pieces,—at sight of which Matilda flushed and smiled, Jerusha laughed, both dropped a quaint little courtesy, plumb down, while their eyes, brighter than the coins, about equalled them in circumference, with the wonder of it.

Friendly good-byes were his portion as he went out with his host to find the ponies just finishing a wrestle with two plump little sheaves of oats.

"Kunnel, I hev n't told you my name; it's—"

"Oh, I know it already, Mr. Spicer; I saw it in your Bible."

"Yes, Heck Spicer; an' my pups is named arter me,—one's Heck and 't other's Spicer."

The old man had said the night before that he must

braid a whip-lash, for the colts had chewed the old one about up. The schoolmaster had purchased a silver-mounted carriage-whip before he left Bodkins, not because he needed it, but for show. He had no use for it whatever, and would never have done much more than affectionately touch a horse with it, unless the animal were securely tied, or had consigned to the knacker. Theophilus, as a sort of parting gift, asked the old man to accept the whip. To be sure, he might quite as appropriately have presented him with an opera-glass. Spicer, to give him his name for once, himself perceived the unfitness of the gift as clearly as if he had a bank account, and he refused it. The schoolmaster insisted, saying, "If Jerusha marries and has a phaeton, give *her* the whip in memory of this time." He never asked himself why he selected Jerusha. Perhaps it was because human nature relishes a bit of amiable mischief now and then.

"That'll do better; but then she'll never hev a—a what did ye call it?—some kind of a kerridge—any more'n I'll hev a pianner. But ef you say so, I'll hev the old woman wind it up in a nice clean cloth, an' I'll put up a peg for 't at the head of our bed, to hang it on agin sich time ez—but that'll never come-and look at it and say, 'Thet's the Kunnel's whip he gin, and we wish the Kunnel luck.' "

In five minutes Theophilus was gone, another "good luck" roared at him as he went.

WALTER MARCH OR SHOEPAC RECOLLECTIONS

ORLANDO B. WILLCOX provided another autobiographical picture of the southern Michigan frontier. Pioneer farmers who had not yet acquired legal title to their holdings were derisively called squatters. They usually were poor, unable to afford even the primitive agricultural equipment then available, and consequently filled the gap with sweat and muscle.

Transforming a plot of virgin timber into a farmstead was backbreaking labor. Long days spent felling trees, dragging trunks to great piles for burning, and rooting out stubborn stumps allowed little time for the comforts of civilization, even if they had been available. The first generation scratched out a meager living as the cultivated fields slowly expanded with each season. A pioneer family could count itself established, when it moved from the first primitive log cabin into a sawn-timber Greek-revival farmhouse.

Orlando Bolivar Willcox was born in Detroit in 1823. He received an appointment to West Point at the age of twenty and graduated 8th in his class in 1847. He saw action during the Mexican War as an artillery officer and fought Indians on the southern and western frontiers. In 1857 Willcox resigned his commission and entered a law practice with his brother in Detroit.

When the Civil War broke out, Willcox was commissioned colonel of the 1st Michigan Infantry. He saw gallant service throughout the war. At Bull Run he was wounded and captured, and he spent more than a year in a southern prison. *Following his exchange in 1862 he won honors at Antietam, Fredericksburg, Knoxville and during the Atlanta campaign. He was promoted to major-general for his distinquished service.*

Following the war he continued his military career, serving in Virginia, San Francisco, Arizona and at other posts. Willcox published two novels under the pen-name, Major March. WALTER MARCH OR SHOEPAC RE—COLLECTIONS appeared in 1856 and was set on the southern Michigan frontier during the days of Willcox's youth.

A Glimpse of Squatter Life

None can describe the sweets of country life,
But those blessed men that do enjoy and taste them.
May's Agrippina

"WHEN will Guilford come home, mamma?" said Mabel, one evening as we were all sitting around the sewing-table.

"I wish, Mabel might tell me," replied my mother. "He grew weary of the apron-strings, I suppose; and became too much of a man for 'chores.'"

"Too much of a man!" exclaimed Mabel, "why, he is only twelve years of age—not much older than Walter, and he never will grow tired of us, I know."

"Twelve years!" said Maud, "he is twelve centuries! Has he not running in his veins all the blood of all the Howards?"

We were laughing at this when the door opened and there appeared an unknown character in a strange costume for our town—not yet opulent enough for beggars. A little old stunted giant in rags, at least out at the elbows and out at the knees, his hat torn on the crown, and slouched over his dirty face. No one recognised this unique personage.

"Friends," came a low voice, "can you give me something to eat and a"—

Here the low voice broke down completely.

"Take off your hat, young sir," said Mrs. March, not knowing what else to say.

The hat was removed.

"Guilford! Guilford!" shouted Mabel, and she ran up to the ragged urchin and threw her arms about his neck.

Mrs. March, too, caught him in her arms and strained him hysterically to her breast. "My boy! my Guilford! my son! what in the world has happened thee? Where have you been? How comes this so?"

"Farming," answered Guilford.

Then he came and sat down between Maud and me in front of the bright fire-place, while Mabel ran out to tell the news to Bowes.

"I have had enough of farming," said Guilford.

"Good! good!" laughed and cried Mabel, who reappeared with Bowes, wiping her hands on her apron again and again. She always did this when excited.

Bowes ran up wildly to her "little man," kissed him and rushed out nearly tearing her apron to pieces. Then Bowes flew away to the cow-yard, shouting

"The little man's come! Brindle, the little man's come!"

And she patted Brindle on the shoulder. But that dignified quadruped vouchsafed no reply. She gave one or two uneasy switches with her tail, and finally tossed her horns wickedly around towards the little crazy woman. And Bowes called her an old thing, or hussy, or something severe, and hurried back to the kitchen, where she found Mabel zealously hunting after some potatoes to put on to roast for the hungry returned prodigal. Then Bowes and Mabel had a very satisfactory talk on the exciting cause of so much stir about the house, and in a little while they came in with cold meat, hot baked Mackinaw potatoes, Bowes's bread, and Brindle's butter.

As soon as he had finished his supper everybody drew near the fire, Bowes and all, to hear Guilford's story. But as he was frequently interrupted, and he himself frequently strayed off in his narration, we shall convey it to the reader in a more straight-forward manner of our own, though the story may suffer by the telling.

Farmer Jumps and Guilford reached the farm-house at about nightfall. The sweet smell of the woods pleased Guilford now in a new sense, he began to feel a sort of proprietorship in it, it was to be his atmosphere.

Great was the manifest surprise of Dame Jumps on beholding our little hero. How a well-dressed city boy should ask her old man Jumps to come out and live on the farm, was a nine days' wonder: she continued all the evening to gaze at him with astonishment.

"Why Jumps, what on airth are you going to do with him?"

"Make a farmer of him."

"Wall, I do declaire! Wall, did you every? Wall, I never!" was all that she could add.

There were three little Jumpses, though one, the eldest, was a pretty long leap, a tall stem of a youth, that looked as if he had sprouted forth in a night. This was Joram Jumps. He was about fourteen years of age. Then came a boy of twelve, and a flaxen-haired limp of a girl of ten. The children seemed to regard Guilford with the wonder of their mother, added to a little awe of their own, and they moved about like mutes, treating their city guest with an occasional stare.

The interior of our beautiful peninsula was but thinly settled, and the country around Farmer Jumps's was almost wilderness. His house was a mere cabin of logs, chinked with a clayey mud, composed of one story, and that contained but the common room in which the family ate, sat, slept, shook with fever and ague, and held periodical prayer meetings for the pioneers of the neighborhood.

Some short cakes were baking in a spider over the coals as Guilford entered. An iron tea-kettle was singing a cheerful welcome and waving its little fleecy banners of steam, and by the time Jumps had turned off the cattle and re-entered, the cabin, was filled with the rich odor of frying pork and potatoes, and Dame Jumps, assisted by her daughter, whose name was Susannah, was setting the table for supper.

The crockery-ware, said Guilford, consisted of the odds and ends of many different old sets, of as many different colors, originally brown, blue, white —even yellow was not wanting. These relics of antiquity were ostentatiously set up, each piece separately, on its edge, on the shelves of a red cupboard. It seems that above everything in the house, except her feather bed, Mrs. Jumps valued her "*cheena*," as she denominated this rubbish of broken wares; and it is a curious fact, that people always bother themselves and fret away their lives on what they foolishly fancy gives them the most happiness. So it was with the dame, as, with a trembling care, Suz handed down the plates, cups, and saucers for the table, her mother fumed and scolded at her, at every turn, lest she should break the cheena.

Before the table was set, Suz had quite fully enlisted, though unknowingly, the sympathy of Guilford. This sympathy was still further excited when all drew up to the table; for when Mrs. Jumps came to pour tea from a black tea-pot with a cover that would be ever coming off, and when Mrs. Jumps deposited sugar in the cups, she put the least in Susannah's—poor Suz was the only one at the table who cared for sugar at all. But Guilford managed so as to give the little pouting girl his own cup. This won her over to him; so that after supper, and she had helped her mother to clear away the dishes, and received the same amount of abuse as before supper, on account of the cheena, she got the two brothers together, and all three of the farmer's children settled around Guilford very sociably for the evening, in the light of the fire, candles being reckoned an extravagance. It may be needless to say what everybody knows—that all town boys are regarded by their country cousins as a sort of superior race. This inly acknowledged superiority, however, the country lads are ever ready to dispute. To Guilford's knowledge, on the occasion before us, these farmer lads were soon ready to defer, for the purpose of more fully extracting information on sundry matters in which they stood in ignorance.

Accordingly Guilford interested them deeply in his accounts of caravans, circuses, militia-trainings, fire engines, skates, schools, kites, tops, jewsharps, and marbles. They were disappointed, however, to find he knew so little about ginger-bread, a goodly array of which, in bird-like, beast-like, man-like, and woman-like forms, they had once seen in a shop window. There had been a lurking disposition at first, on the part of the young Jumpses, to humble my brother next day—so Susannah afterwards revealed;—but his frankness, and the satisfactory information he gave, on the whole, changed their intentions; and far from desiring now to expose his ignorance of the various secrets of woodcraft, they resolved to aid him all in their power to learn farming. As for Suz, she was perfectly charmed, as she told me long afterwards, with his gentleness and superior understanding. To her, Guilford was of a new order of being,

and at once she began to "slick up," as she said.

Then bed-time came. Guilford had observed but one bed, and wondered whether Jumps and his wife and family and he were all to sleep in it. But Mrs. Jumps soon solved that problem, by drawing from beneath the bedstead a truckle bed large enough to hold the three boys; and a couch was made for Susannah on a long blue chest—which, by the way, had probably held their worldly goods and chattels when they emigrated from Vermont.

Mr. Jumps being the last to retire, blew out the light, that is to say, covered up the fire, leaving the hearth in sole possession of a speckled cat, and a pan of buckwheat batter, placed there to "rise" for breakfast. But no sooner did silence prevail in the loghouse, than Guilford heard a long dismal howl, that arose from the woods in the midst of which they lay. Soon came another, longer, and mingled with fellow-howls, each one seeming to draw nigher and nigher to the door, till at length it seemed to be besieged with a roar of dismal howlings.

Guilford drew the coverlid over his head; but his bedfellows only laughed at his fears. Ashamed of betraying himself in such wise to these country bumpkins, he uncovered his head. A perfect blast of roars and threats, mingled with whines and screeches of disappointed yet greedy rage saluted his ears.

"What is it?" demanded he in a whisper.

"Nothing but wolves. Go to sleep."

"How do you like country music, boy?" asked Mrs. Jumps, with a coarse laugh.

Mr. Jumps interposed now, and soothed the alarm of Guilford by telling him that the animals were of a small, harmless sort, and though they had howled, apparently, at the door every night since he had squatted there, yet on getting up to drive them away he never found them anywhere near, so that now the family took no notice of them.

At daybreak the household was astir. Guilford arose with his bedfellows, and Mr. Jumps set him at once to work. He was dispatched with Tobias, or Toby, as they called the younger lad, after the cows. They were soon found, and easily driven home; but Guilford returned with his feet and legs wet to the knees in the heavy dew. Then he assisted Joram at chopping wood for the house, so that breakfast-time found him already fatigued. Even Susannah laughed a little at his pale looks, but soon checked herself, for fear of breaking a piece of the yellow cheena she was taking from its throne on the red cupboard. My brother was not at all discouraged; he had a stout heart, and breakfast refreshed him. After the morning meal, all went to a small clearing not far from the house—not more than forty acres of the Jumps estate was as yet under cultivation. The work before them now was *follering,* as the squatters called it, or clearing the land of felled trees or brushwood. Serviceable logs were drawn off, and that which was left they gathered into great heaps, and set on fire. Jumps and Joram busied themselves with the logs, and made the woods ring again with the blows of their axes, and the sound of their voices as they shouted over the oxen.

When dinner-time came, Dame Jumps appeared in the angel avocation of blowing a trumpet—that is to say sounding a long tin horn. She showed herself at the corner of the cabin, and with the instrument applied to her mouth with one hand, while the other arm she held akimbo at her side to assist in the mighty effort, she brayed forth a Jericho-shaking blast. There was no resisting this call, it said in Mrs. Jump's most decided manner:

"Dinner's ready, and waits for no man."

Guilford was hungry and ate heartily. He deserved some reward for his plight. His hands were scratched, his face blackened, and his eyes filled up with cinders. Suz expressed her sympathy by bringing a tin washbasin, and water—none of the cleanest—from a spring near by the house, distilling through the black vegetable mould into a barrel which was half alive with insects, while occasionally, a lingering frog who had come up to sun his body out of the torpor of an October day, plumped himself down with a splash as you approached.

After dinner the party betook themselves to the clearing again, where they worked away till near nightfall, when Toby and Guilford were again dispatched for the cows; no trifling errand, as the animals wandered far during the day—water in the woods being plenty—and the boys were both fatigued.

And the evenings, how different at Green Run from our sweet, quiet, yet lively evenings in the library at home!

The good humor and refinement of my mother, the high-toned, soft spoken morality of Maud, the incessant raillery of Mabel; these were exchanged for the blunt good sense of Mr. Jumps, the trumpet clangor of Mrs. Jumps, and the vacant wonderment of the young Jumpses.

A fortnight or more the male inhabitants of the cabin were engaged in the clearing, during which time the fatigues were too great to admit of much conversation at night. On some very pleasant evenings, however, the fascinating Indian summer atmosphere would tempt them to sit out in front of the door, one on a bench, another on the stump of a log, and while the evening came on, soothed into quiet by the chirrup of the cricket, and the monotonous drone of the tree toad, and lit up by the fireflies in the bush, Jumps would hush the ever prevailing complaints of his wife, and the stupid questionings of his sons, and moralize learnedly over his pipe to the more intelligent Guilford.

"If I weren't a farmer, I never would be one; no, its the last calling on airth for a man in this country. Now here's my boys and that gal, what do they know? hardly enough to come in when it rains. Now, let me advise you to adopt a course."

"Yes sir," said Guilford, "what course would you adopt, Mr. Jumps?"

"Wall, every man that gits tired doin anything else, or breaks down in life, always thinks he can make a farmer of himself, just as easy as rollin off a log, but it ain't so tarnal easy. A man ought to have a turn for it, with a constitution like a horse. He must work like a dog, and be weather-wise as the Prophet Elijah. And that ain't all nuther—he must adopt a course."

"Yes sir," said Guilford—who knew already that 'to adopt a course," was the Jumps philosophy—his panacea for every ill. Jumps rarely condescends to explain himself after uttering this indisputable dogma. And so now, he arose, entered the house to rekindle his pipe, and reappeared with a live coal, which he shifted rapidly from his right hand to his left, and as swiftly from his left hand to his right, vainly endeavoring to plant it in the bowl. The refractory coal dropped on the floor. Jumps took the tongs to it.

"Yes!" resumed the smoking philosopher, "a man may

think he knows all about farming and get his fingers burnt after all. Now if it weren't for fear of going through the woods like an over particular gal and taking up with a crooked stick after all, I'd change my"—

At this moment Joram broke in.

"Dad, don't you think I'd make a smart minister of the gospel?"

Mr. Jumps, senior, did not reply. He rose up hastily, knocked the ashes from the bowl of his pipe on the nail of his thumb, went in the cabin, covered up the fire, and— went to bed.

"Every fool thinks he can be a preacher, too," quoth Guilford to himself.

Guilford was not too young to perceive some of the hopeful peculiarities of thought and feeling among the squatters.

First, they were of the opinion that their lot in life was a little the hardest on the face of the earth.

Second, to vex the patient souls of this primitive people, there must always needs be something wrong in the daily course of events—peculiarly theirs to suffer— the world around them of course exempt, as everybody else's world always is, and always was, of a *couleur de rose*.

The cow was always dry; the ox always wanted shoeing; an utensil was always broke, or a neighbor had borrowed it just when it was wanted; the weather never suited the crops, and the crops neither suited the weather nor came up to their expectations; there never was time to do what was required to be done *now;* Mrs. Jumps thought she worked herself to death, and had no comforts; Susannah was always out of shoes, and yet *would* wear them, though they cost a fortune; the boys wanted jack-knives, jewsharps, new caps, and school-books—they never could be prevailed upon to study when they got them. In short, Mr. and Mrs. Jumps had left the pleasant-est home, the dearest friends, the most lucrative busi-ness, the best schools, the grayest parson, and the greenest hills, at home in good old *Vairmount*, to come to *Michigan*, where they had no neighbors, no parson, no hills, and the children were growing up without educa-tion, they were all working themselves *to* death, and, after all, didn't seem to get on. With reference to the last complaint, we may as well anticipate a few years, and state, that notwithstanding this melancholy list of grievances, the Jumpses continued to exist, nay, to thrive, from year to year, till, as we shall see, in due time, they had the best farm in the county, and the Jumpses became one of the "first families."

Guilford observed this very satisfactory account, which it gave them such evident delight to draw, and thought that as it is only necessary to see an evil in order to avoid falling into it ourselves, he himself would do better; therefore, he continued to hold on steadily to his course.

But Mr. Jumps seemed to take a peculiar pleasure in making Guilford March work.

"You have adopted a course, my little fellow," he would say, "and you must stick to it through thick and thin."

Accordingly, there was little peace or rest for the poor boy, until night came. He began to fancy himself growing dull, like Joram and Toby. The thought horrified him; yet all the boys he saw were of the same species. "All work and no play makes Jack a dull boy," sure enough, thought he.

There were a hundred people in the vicinity—two-thirds of them were down with ague or bilious fever.

The nearest neighbors to Farmer Jumps were the O'Gradys. They lived a mile down the creek or run, whose greenish, vegetable color, gave name to this neighborhood. They were Irish; had been in better circumstances, they said, as all old country people, I believe, do say. Whether they descended from the King O'Grady I never have learned, but I dare say they did.

At any rate, their descent was very great, as both husband and wife got drunk, and frightened Guilford more than once with their dreadful oaths and beastly conduct.

It was some time in December that an incident happened in the O'Grady family, which, added to what had already been preying upon the sensitive youth's feelings, was the means of his leaving the detestable precincts of Green Run.

The terrible event haunted his imagination day and night, and gave a horrible significance to the howling of the wolves.

He took sudden flight one morning when he had been

sent after the cows, without Tobias, who had cut his foot. He left his best suit of clothes behind him, with the secret of his flight, in Susannah's keeping, and appeared before us in the manner already related.

My mother's plan for curing Guilford of a desire for farm-life had succeeded—aided as it was by fortuitous circumstances, of which the good lady never had dreamed.

"My son, you will go to school to-morrow."

"Yes, my dear mother, as soon as I have wood enough chopped to last Bowes all day."

THE PUDDLEFORD PAPERS

SICKNESS often compounded the primitive living conditions, isolation and long hours of toil experienced by Michigan pioneers. Typhoid, diptheria and other now conquered diseases killed entire families, and periodic choleria epidemics ravaged the frontier. Doctors rode circuit among the wilderness settlements, but primitive treatments ranging from bleeding to massive doses of mercury compounds often did more harm than good.

Few pioneers escaped a bout with the ague. "The Shakes", as pioneers called the disease, featured alternate periods of fever and chills. The ague seldom proved fatal but temporarily disabled entire communities. Pioneers adjusted their schedules to well days and ague days. The time for court days, shop hours and house raisings revolved around the ague's daily dictums.

Frontiersmen developed numerous and imaginative theories to account for the disease. Some thought it came from the newly turned sod, others from rotting vegetation, and still others from damp night air. But pioneers noted one thing for certain; the ague was more prevelant near swampy locales. They little suspected that the true cause of the ague, or malaria as it eventually came to be known, was the hordes of mosquitoes that bred in the stagnant swamp waters. When farmers drained the swamps for agricultural reasons and mosquitoes grew less numerous, the ague disappeared in Michigan.

Henry H. Riley was born in Great Barrington, Massachusetts in 1813. Orphaned at the age of ten, he served an apprenticeship on a New York newspaper, and began editing a paper in Waterloo, New York in 1837. He *sold out in 1842 and moved to Kalamazoo. After studying law for six months, he set up practice in Constantine where he resided until his death in 1888. Judge Riley served as St. Joseph County Prosecuting Attorney and represented southwestern Michigan in the state senate in 1850 and 1862.*

In the early 1850's Riley began contributing a series of comical sketches about pioneer life in Constantine to the KNICKERBOCKER MAGAZINE. These articles earned him a national following, and he published then as a book, PUDDLEFORD AND ITS PEOPLE, in 1854. This Michigan classic was revised and reprinted in various editions throughout the nineteenth century. Judge Riley gives us a glimpse of how the ague affected the residents of early Constantine.

Puddleford And Its People

The 'Fev' Nag'—Conflicting Theories—'Oxergin and Hydergin'—Teazle's Rationale—The Scourge of the West—Sile Bates, and his Condition—Squire Long-bow, and Jim Buzzard—Puddleford Prostrate—Various Practitioners—'The Billerous Duck'—Pioneer Martyrs—Wave over Wave.

DURING my first fall's residence at Puddleford, I frequently heard a character spoken of, who seemed to be full as famous in the annals of the place as Squire Long-bow himself. He was called by a great variety of names, and very seldom alluded to with respect. He was termed the 'Fev-Nag,' the 'Ag-an-Fev,' the 'Shakin' Ager,' the 'Shakes,' and a great variety of other hard names were visited upon him.

That he was the greatest scourge Puddleford had to contend with, no one denied. Who he really was, what he was, where born, and for what purpose, was a question. Dobbs had one theory, Short another, and Teazle still another. Dr. Dobbs said 'that his appearance must be accounted for in this wise—that the marshes were all covered with water in the Spring, that the sun began to grow so all-fir'd hot 'long 'bout July and August, that it cream'd over the water with a green scum, and rotted the grass, and this all got stewed inter a morning fog, that rose up and elated itself among the Ox-er-gin and Hy-der-gin, and pizened every body it touched.'

Dr. Dobbs delivered this opinion at the public house, in a very oracular style. I noticed several Puddlefordians in his presence at the time, and before he closed, their jaws dropped, and their gaping mouths and expanded eyes were fixed upon him with wonder.

Dr. Teazle declared that 'Dobbs didn't know any thing about it. He said the ager was buried up in the airth, and that when the sile was turned up, it got loose, and folks breath'd it into their lungs and from the lungs it went into the liver, and from the liver it went to the kidneys, and the secretions got fuzzled up, and the bile turn'd black, and the blood didn't run, and it set every body's inards all a-tremblin'.'

Without attempting the origin of the ague and fever, it was, and always has been the scourge of the West. It is the foe that the West has ever had to contend with. It delays improvement, saps constitutions, shatters the whole man, and lays the foundation for innumerable diseases that follow and finish the work for the grave. It is not only ague and fever that so seriously prostrates the pioneer; but the whole family of intermittent and remittent fevers, all results of the same cause, press in to destroy. Perhaps no one evil is so much dreaded. Labor, privation, poverty are nothing in comparison. It is, of course, fought in a great variety of ways, and the remedies are as numerous as they are ridiculous. A physician who is really skillful in the treatment of these diseases is, of course, on the road to wealth, but skillful physicians were not frequent in Puddleford, as the reader has probably discovered.

I recollect that during the months of September and October, subsequently to my arrival, all Puddleford was 'down,' to use the expression of the country; and if the reader will bear with me, and pledge himself not to accuse me of trifling with so serious a subject, I will endeavor to describe Puddleford 'in distress.'

I will premise by saying that it is expected that persons who are on their feet during these visitations, give up their time and means to those who are not. There is a nobleness of soul in a western community in this respect, that does honor to human nature. A village is one great family—every member must be provided for—old grudges are, for the time, buried.

I have now a very vivid remembrance of seeing Sile Bates, one bright October morning, walking through the main street of Puddleford, at the pace of a funeral procession, his old winter overcoat on, and a faded shawl tied about his cheeks. Sile informed me 'that he believed the ager was comin' on-ter him—that he had a spell on't the day before, and the day before that—that he had been a-stewin' up things to break the fits, and clean out his constitution, but it stuck to him like death on-ter a nigger'— he said 'his woman and two boys were shakin' like all possess't, and he rally believed if some body didn't stop it, the log cabin would tumble down round their ears.' He said 'there warn't nobody to do nuthin' 'bout house, and that all the neighbors were worse off than he was.'

Sile was a melancholy object indeed. And in all conscience, reader, did you ever behold so solemn, wobegone a thing on the round earth, as a man undergoing the full merits of ague and fever? Sile sat down on a barrel and commenced gaping and stretching, and now and then dropped a remark expressive of his condition. He finally began to chatter, and the more he chattered, the more ferocious he waxed. He swore 'that if he ever got well, he'd burn his house, sell his traps, 'bandon his land, pile his family into his cart, hitch on his oxen, and drive 'em, and drive 'em to the north pole, where there warn't no ager, he knew. One minit,' he said, 'he was a-freezin', and then he was a-burnin', and then he was a-sweatin' to death, and then he had a well day, and that didn't 'mount to nothin', for the critter was only gettin' strength to jump on him agin the next.' Sile at last exhausted himself, and getting upon his feet went off muttering and shaking toward his house.

The next man I met was Squire Longbow. The Squire was moving slower, if possible, than Bates. His face looked as if it had been just turned out of yellow oak, and his eyes were as yellow as his face. As the Squire never surrendered to any thing, I found him not disposed to surrender to ague and fever. He said 'he'd only had a little brush, but he'd knock it out on-him in a day or two. He was jist goin' out to scrape some elder bark *up*, to act as

74

an emetic, as Aunt Sonora said if he scraped it *down,* it would have t'other effect—and that would kill it as dead as a door-nail.'

I soon overhauled Jim Buzzard, lying half asleep in the bottom of his canoe, brushing off flies with an oak branch. Jim, too, was a case, but it required something more than sickness to disturb his equilibrium. Jim said 'he warn't sick, but he felt the awfullest tired any dog ever did—he was the all-thunderest cold t'other day, *he* ever was in hot weather—somethin' 'nother came on-ter him all of a suddint, and set his knees all goin and his jaws a quiv'rin', and so he li'd down in-ter the sun, but the more he li'd, the more he kept on a shakin', and then that are all went off agin, and he'd be darned to gracious, if he did n't think he'd burn up—and so he just jumped inter the river, and cool'd off—and, now he feel'd jist so agin—and so he'd got where the sun could strike him a little harder this time. What shall a feller do?' at last inquired Jim.

'Take medicine,' said I.

'Not by a jug-full,' said Jim. 'Them are doctors do n't get any of their stuff down my throat. If I can't stand it as long as the ager, then I'll give in. Let-er-shake if it wants to—it works harder than I do, and will get tir'd bym-by. Have you a little plug by-yer jest now, as I have n't had a chew sin' morning, as it may help a feller some?' Jim took the tobacco, rolled over in his canoe, gave a grunt, and composed himself for sleep.

This portrait of Buzzard would not be ludicrous, if it was not true. Whether Socrates or Plato, or any other heathen philosopher, has ever attempted to define this kind of happiness, is more than I can say. In fact, reader, I do not believe that there was one real Jim Buzzard in the whole Grecian republic.

But why speak of individual cases? Nearly all Puddleford was prostrate—man, woman, and child. There were a few exceptions, and the aid of those few was nothing compared to the great demand of the sick. It was providential that the nature of the disease admitted of one well day, because there was an opportunity to 'exchange works,' and the sick of to-day could assist the sick of tomorrow, and so *vice versa.*

I looked through the sick families, and found the pa-

tients in all conditions. One lady had 'just broke the ager on-to her by sax-fax tea, mix'd with Columbo.' Another 'had been a-tryin' eli-cum-paine and pop'lar bark, but it did n't lie good on her stomach, and made her 'eny most crazy.' Another woman was 'so as to be crawlin','—another was 'getting quite peert'—another 'could n't keep any thing down, she felt so qualmy'—another said, 'the disease was runnin' her right inter the black janders, and then she *was* gone'—another had 'run clear of yesterday's chill, and was now going to weather it,' and so on, through scores of cases.

It is worthy of note, the popular opinion of the character of this disease. Although Puddleford had been afflicted with it for years, yet it was no better understood by the mass of community than it was at first. I have already given the opinion of Dobbs and Teazle of the *causes* of the ague; but as Dobbs and Teazle held entirely different theories, Puddleford was not much enlightened by their wisdom. (If some friend will inform me when and where any community was ever enlightened by the *united* opinion of its physicians, I will publish it in my next work.) Aunt Sonora had a theory which was a little old, but it was her's, and she had a right to it. She said 'no body on airth could live with a stomach full of bile, and when the shakin' ager come on, you'd jest got-ter go to work and get off all the bile—bile *was* the ager, and physicians might talk to her till she was gray, 'bout well folks having bile—she know'd better—'t warn't no such thing.'

Now Aunt Sonora practised upon this theory, and the excellent old lady administered a cart-load of boneset every season—blows to elevate the bile, and the leaf as a tonic. However erroneous her theory might have been, I am bound to say that her practice was about as successful as that of the regular physician.

Mr. Beagle declared 'that the ague was in the blood, and the patient must first get rid of all his bad blood, and then the ager would go along with it.' Swipes said 'it was all in the stomach.' Dobbs said 'the billerous duck chok'd up with the mash fogs, and the secretions went every which way, and the liver got as hard as sole-leather, and the patient becom' sick, and the ager set in, and then the fever, and the hull system got-er goin' wrong, and if it warn't stopped, natur'd give out, and the man would die.' Teazle said 'it com'd from the plough'd earth, and got inter the air, and jist so long as folks breath'd aguery air, jist so long they'd have the ager.' Turtle said 'the whole tribe on 'em, men-doctors and women-doctors, were blockheads, and the surest way to get rid of the ager, was to let it run, and when it had run itself out, it would stop, and not afore.'

Here then, was Puddleford, at the mercy of a dozen theories, and yet men and women recovered, when the season had run its course, and were tolerably sure of health, until another year brought around another instalment of miasma.

How many crops of men have been swept off by the malaria of every new western country, I will not attempt to calculate! How many, few persons have ever attempted! This item very seldom goes into the cost of colonization. Pioneers are martyrs in a sublime sense, and it is over their bones that school-houses, churches, colleges, learning, and refinement are finally planted. But the death of a pioneer is a matter of no moment in our country—it is almost as trifling a thing as the death of a soldier in an Indian fight. There is no glory to be won on any such field. One generation rides over another, like waves over waves, and 'no such miserable interrogatory,' as Where has it gone? or How did it go? is put; but What did it do?—What has it left behind?

Any one who has long been a resident in the West, must have noticed the operation of climate upon the constitution. The man from the New-England mountains, with sinews of steel, soon finds himself flagging amid western miasma, and a kind of stupidity creeps over him, that it is impossible to shake off. The system grows torpid, the energies die, indifference takes possession, and thus he vegetates—he does not live.

And, dear reader, it does not lighten the bloom of the picture, to find Dobbs, and Teazle, and Short quarrelling over the remains of some departed one, endeavoring to delude the public into something themselves have no conception of, about the manner in which he or she went out of the world. Not that all the physicians are Dobbses or Teazles, but these sketches are written away out on the rim of society, the rim of Western society, where the townships are not yet all organized, and a sacred regard to truth compels me to record facts as they exist.

THE WILDERNESS AND THE ROSE

PIONEER town developers chose their sites with an eye for transportation. Ideal locations were on navigable rivers or at the junction of several Indian trails. When iron rails began snaking their way west from Detroit the frontier suddenly ended and boom days began for those villages in their path. The route the railroads took, as we shall find out in the selection from THE WILDERNESS AND THE ROSE, was not always determined by geographic considerations.

The first railroad west of Schenectady, New York, the Erie and Kalamazoo, was incorporated in 1833. By 1836 a set of rails made of white oak with a strap of iron nailed on top stretched the 32 miles from Toledo to Adrian. Horse drawn coaches went into operation that year, and in 1837 the first locomotive west of the Alleghanies puffed along, showering passengers with sparks and cinders. Burn holes in clothing were an inconvenience, but "snake-heads," caused when the iron strap rail broke loose and curled up through the floor of the car, endangered life and limb.

During the 1840's the Erie and Kalamazoo Railroad built branch lines including the one described in the following selection. Keene still exists as a tiny hamlet known as Keene Corners, and Lanesville is present day Hudson, a name the Lenewee County community adopted in 1840. The Erie and Kalamazoo Railroad eventually became a part of the Lake Shore and Michigan Southern Railroad.

Jerome James Wood published THE WILDERNESS AND THE ROSE in Hudson in 1890. Wood wrote about the early development of the region in which he had grown up and lived all his life. The book is weak in plot but strong in local color and well worth reading as a source of pioneer history.

The Iron Horse

"On through the darkness with thundering footsteps,
On through the hush and the silence of night,
Labors the engine, wile steady before her
Gleams clear and radiant the beams of her light."
A.B. Bragdon

IN the spring great activity prevailed in Keene. An intense excitement stirred the settlers. The tide of migration westward demanded better facilities for transportation. The Southern railroad was projecting its line west of Adrian; already the surveyors had reached Keene.

"I tell yeou what, eour fortun's made th' minit that road strikes this plice," Brother Jonathan said with emphasis.

"The Lord has deemed it best to send this blessin' to us," said Deacon Jones.

"Corner lots'll go a whoopin'er I'm no jedge," the little justice said.

"This is altogether th' most excitin' time since th' war of eighteen twelve," chimed Peg-leg Brown.

"I've heern tell they was a running 'nother line 'bout ten miles south through Lane," Brother Jonathan said.

"Tain't no good, though, this yere Keene's right in th' direct line west of Adrian."

" 'N Lanesville, what does that little, stinkin' place amount to anyway?"

"They don't stand no show at all."

"Th' nat'ral 'vantages of this place's too great for that."

"They mount just's well hang up their fiddle."

"Jest's sure's you live."

"Imagine th' consequence this 'ere place'll be," Brother Jonathan suggested.

"All owin' to an overpowerin' providence," the Deacon said.

"There's no knowin' what them Lanesville fellers will be up to, though."

"Sho, I ain't a bit afeerd o' them."

"Whar's this 'ere road agoin' to?"

"Tew Kalamazoo er Checawgo."

"They say that Checawgo, or Chicogo, as some calls it, is destined to be a great city."

"Th' liveliest place in the' West now, by all odds."

'Built right in er swamp, too."

"Medina's th' smartest place I know on in these parts. They've got a store thar that does more business than th' rest o' th' country put together an' now they've started a mill, too, an' they come from 'way down in Ohio an' Indiany to git their grists ground."

"I thought Canandaigua had got th' start of 'em."

"Oh, git out! They are a movin' th' houses from Canandaig' to Medina."

"And Morenci, how about her?"

"Morenci an' all th' rest o' em'll 'mount to nothin' when th' railroad gits to Keene."

Immigration was coming into the country at a lively rate. Stages from the railroad terminus at Adrian were laden with passengers seeking homes and fortunes in the New West. Business at the Franklin tavern was booming. The new era of prosperity had set in. The advent of the railroad would be the clincher to make Keene a commercial mart of prominence. It would soon be at high tide.

The promoters of the rival, Lanesville, were not idle, however. A leading light of the place had a confidential talk with one of the engineers running the line for the railroad. The Lanesville man was a shrewd chap, ready to drive a sharp bargain.

He said to the surveyor: "Now you might jest's well come in out o' th' wet an' take care o' yourself in locatin' this 'ere railroad o' yourn."

"Yes, but how can I deflect the line two miles south to get to Lanesville; we're making for Hillsdale now, and that's even farther north than Keene is?"

"But if we made it an object to ye, an' got it run through here as th' most feasible route, in your eye, you ought to do it an' look out fer yourself."

"What sort of a condition would you make?"

"Make it in corner lots, right here in th' heart o' th' town, an' if th' railroad comes it's bound to be a city, an' yer fortune's made sure fire."

"I think I can see some advantages about the place that I never saw before," the engineer said.

"That's it, that's it, work yer courage up an' go in.

These corner lots's yours when th' road's here."

It was an infinite astonishment to the inhabitants of Keene when it was soon after announced that the railroad would go through Lanesville.

"That beats all creation," said Brother Jonathan.

"A cross we'll have to bear," said Deacon Jones.

"Something beyond my jurisdiction," the little justice said.

"This air road'll be as crooked as a ram's horn," said Coonskin Joe.

"Th' greatest disap'intment to me since Long Tom 'scaped th' clutches of th' law," said Peg-leg Brown.

"What shall we do in th' midst of th' 'fliction?" the Deacon said.

"wa-al, neow, if th' mountain won't go tew Mahomet, why, by th' beard of th' prophit, Mahomet will go tew th' mountain. I'll move; I'm 'bout Yankee 'nough fer that," Brother Jonathan said.

"What, move yer hotel to Lanesville?"

"Sartin."

"How?"

"Jest put th' buildin' on skids, an' th' oxen'll yank it over there. Ther'll be no interruption of business."

"An keep tavern by th' way?"

"Ya-as. It'll be th' wayside inn."

"Haw-haw! haw-haw!"

"I'll bet a York shilling there's a nigger in th' woodpile somewhere."

"How's that?"

"In gitting this road to Lanesville."

Mr. Bony Jenks spoke up and said; "I heerd a man say as how if this 'ere railroad come through here they'd ship everything out o' th' country, an' butter, eggs an' sich'd be scarcer'n hens' teeth, an' thar wouldn't be nothin' left fer th' folks to eat, 'twould be so tarnal scarce an' dear. Seemed to me like th' man what said it was clean agin us, an' arter all thar' 'pears to be suthin like sense in what he says."

"Sho," said old man Brown, the store-keeper, "I take jest an opposite view, an opposite view entirely. Here we've come into this country to raise stuff, an' if th' railroad comes an' does all th' haulin' what'll th' hosses an' oxen have to do, I'd like to know? An' if there ain't nothing' for th' hosses to do what'll be th' use of raisin' hay an' all that kind o' fodder when th' country's cleared up? I tell you there's somethin' to look at in that direction."

"Yeou git eout," Brother Jonathan said, "when th' railroad comes this country'll be *developed* an' no mistake. We've just got tew git on th' line of *development* at Lanesville. This 'ere hull settlement's got to git thar pritty quick."

"A-a-me, brother!" drawled the Deacon.

Brother Jonathan was as good as his word. It being definitely determined that the railroad would go through Lanesville, he made preparations for removing his tavern to the coming metropolis. The question of location agitated the inn-keeper.

"I've half a notion tew locate my—er hotel on th' main corners on th' east side o' the crick, Lovina."

"Hotel, hotel," repeated Mrs. Bellamy, "'pears tew me it's gittin' pritty stylish for plain folks like us that's allers kep' a tavern tew be talkin' 'bout hotels."

"Wa-al, we mount jest's well begin fust's last. Here's this 'ere Lanesville goin' tew be a great city, an' eour hotel'll be th' fust an' most important one. We'll be there all ready tew greet th' railroad when she comes; so we've got tew put on some style, th' occasion demands it."

"There's suthin in that, but it seems tew me that th' west side'd be th' best; most places is grow'd up on the west side of th' streams, I don't know why."

"S'pose it's on account of westward th' star of empire's takin' it's way. Gits to goin' an' can't stop till it gits clear across th' crick; but here at Lanesville th' cars'll take wood an' water on th' east side, an' there's where th' town'll be, else I'm no prophet or th' son of one, an' there's where I'll set my stakes. They think they're some punkins there already. Last week, at th' shootin' match on th' flats, old Si Hawks put up th' chickens an' turkeys. Hank Stump an' Bill Flint was there a matchin' pennies on th' head of a bar'l, th' same slick game they played on th' natives at Rollin an' Coontown. They was pards, of course. Their onderhanded game was to use double-headed pennies. In throwin' or matchin' on th' head of a bar'l, the coppers had tew be picked up by one of the pards. If it was played on a board, or table, the coin could be brushed off by any of the players and the deception diskivered. If yeou see 'em a matchin' pennies 'round the head of a bar'l, look out for 'em sartin' sure; these pards is a linin' their pockets with "Bungtown coppers." Neow, tain't for me to give it away. I'm in the hotel biz, an' depend somewhat on th' entire public.

"How kin men do like that an' be respectable?"

"If yeou get th' money yeou'll be respectible anyhow. Some men are up tew all sorts o' tricks. Why there's Bony Jenks, who's traveled all over New York an' New Jersey, so they say, an' he was took in the slickest way ever heerd of. He was agoin' along th' road tew Coontown one day when he noticed a chap a practicin' turnin' some walnut shells a top of a stump. It looked so simple-like that it 'tracted Bony's 'tention an' th' innocent an' lamb-like stranger 'splained tew him that 'twas suthin' he'd seen deoun East, an' he was a practicin' tew do it himself. Th' thing was to tell which shell th' ball was under an' at th' same time he awkwarly showed th' little joker under the shell. As scarce as change was with Bony, he says, "Bet yew four shillin' I kin tell, an' the stranger he covered Bony's money. An' when our feller citizen lifted th' cup th' joker war'm't there. He had picked up the wrong walnut shell, an' was terribly cut up at bein' taken in an' done for by so green a lookin' stranger who was evidently layin' for suckers."

"How was it done?"

"Entirely by slight o' hand. There's ever so many skin-games what seem tew thrive in a new country. There's th' strap game an' three-card monte, all calculated to deceive th' onwary."

"I don't see how they find victims."

"Oh, they allers find someone who thinks they knows more'n they do, but I'll tell yeou what, an' it's th' result of life-long observation an' 'sperience, yeou bet yeou life it never pays tew bet on another man's game."

"I shall worry th' life out o' me a thinkin' that yeou are liable tew git me into all sorts o' trouble by fallin' into these traps sot for the onwary."

"Tut, tut, woman," said the landlord, and he went out of doors whistling and his spouse restored her amiability somewhat by saying: 'Th' sins o' this life, as th' preacher said, are visited on th' sons of men. I'm thankful it don't take in th' wimmen, tew."

Brother Jonathan got his hotel building up on skids and rollers. By hitching log-chains to the underpinning of the building it was all ready to move being, virtually a house on wheels. According to previously concerted arrangement his old friends and neighbors, when the preparations were all made, were on hand in force with ox-teams to haul the caravansary to its new location down the valley.

"Haw, Buck! haw, Buck, haw! Gee up, Bright! gee up, gee! were the commands of Deacon Jones as he maneuvered his bovines into place, with a large ox-goad plying over their heads.

"The Deacon wouldn't part with them steers for nothin'," said Bony Jenks.

So wonted had the landlord become to the spot where he had set his stakes that he was taking a farewell view of the surroundings, and was interrupted in the communion with himself by old Brown, the store-keeper, who sadly exclaimed: "This seems kinder tough to have thisere settlement broke up, but if you go, I go too. It's one go, all go, sheep."

"They say th' school-teacher's goin' into business at Lanesville," the Deacon said.

"Suthin' tuggin' at his heart-strings to draw him thar. Don't know but I'll be inclined to go myself," the little justice said.

"Wal, if th' court goes, I goes too; b'sides, I think that gal's had an attachment served on her by th' school-master, an' I want to see it satisfied," said Peg-leg Brown.

Deeming these remarks to be of a personal nature, the landlord did not deign to notice them and merely said, in a general way: "Wa-al, we shall leave th' road behind us an' will be glad tew see ye all come. One thing's sartin, th' latch-string of th' Franklin House'll allers be hanging eout for yeou."

The journey down the road to Lanesville was a unique one. The cattle tugged and pulled at the command of the drivers; the chains creaked and the timbers snapped, but it was fairly easy work for the united oxen; and, though they halted often, the task was finally done. As the building was moved up on the new site all hands united in a hearty cheer, joined in also by the residents of Lanesville, who had been attracted to the spot.

The landlord's family had retained possession of the building while it was in transit, and, by the time that the teams were unhitched, Mrs. Bellamy and her pretty daughter, Matilda, aided by the hostler, passed a luncheon of cider and doughnuts to the party constituting the moving-bee.

Cup in hand, Deacon Jones mounted a stump, conveniently at hand, and holding his glass aloft, said: "Here's to Brother Jonathan, who knows how to keep a hotel,his good wife an' pritty dorter; here's long life and prosperity to them, and to th' Franklin House."

"Drink hearty, boys, drink hearty!" exclaimed the open-hearted boniface, from his inmost soul.

"Here's to 'em all," said the crowd in unison, and the new house was christened.

"When I git things straightened around a bit, I want all yeou bous tew come an' see us. We'll have a shake-down— a reg'lar old'fashioned time," the landlord said.

"You bet your boots we will," they said.

The new hotel was ready for business none too soon, for gangs of men were already putting up trestle work for the track across the river-bottoms, and other gangs were approaching the place from the East, grading and clearing the way for the laying of the strap-rail used in the days of primitive railroading.

When this was accomplished and the stringers, upon which the strap-rail was to be laid, were down, it was discovered that the supply of the latter article would reach only to Clayton. Here was a dilemma, indeed. It would be months before another supply could be secured. The inhabitants of Lanesville, as well as the constructors of the road, were impatient at the delay. The inventive ingenuity of man ever keeps the adage good, that where there's a will there's a way.

"Seems tew infernal bad that this 'ere road is tied up an' won't be able to git here this year," the landlord said.

"Wal, I dunno 'bout that, I've got an idea; think I'll see th' boss. I b'lieve we kin git some hard-maple strips at th' saw-mill, an' spike 'em on in place of th' strap-rail fer th' keers to run on, an' it'll answer every purpose," a carpenter engaged on the trestle-work said.

When he approached the superintendent with the

project, he readily fell in with the plan, and it was speedily put into execution.

"Hang me, if I didn't think we'd have an exasperatin' delay," said the official.

The experiment proved successful. Amid the plaudits of the small, but excited populace, the "Comet," with two coaches attached, steamed into Lanesville. It was a diminutive affair, we would say now, and would compare with a threshing engine of to-day; but, nevertheless, 'twas the pioneer of the mighty engines that now speed across the continent.

Excitement was at its greatest height when the train rolled up in front of the Franklin House. Peg-leg Brown stood near the track. He was infected with enthusiasm, and swung his hat wildly in the air. He shouted: "Saw my leg off short! Clar th' track, th' bulgine's comin'! All git aboard for Pittsford, Osseo an' Hillsdale; if you can't git aboard git a slab!"

THE RED KEGGERS

THE task of converting the Michigan wilderness into productive farmsteads allowed little time for social amenities. Weddings, funerals and hellfire and brimstone sermons preached by Methodist circuit riders brought pioneers together and helped relieve the isolation. Communal work-related projects provided other social functions. An unwritten law of the frontier decreed that pioneers pool their efforts to accomplish difficult tasks. Corn huskings, harvest parties and house and barn raisings allowed men to demonstrate their skill as artisans and women their finesse in the kitchen. Young couples might also begin their courting.

Eugene Thwing takes us to a pioneer house raising in the Midland area in the selection from THE RED KEGGERS. His faithful portrayal of the occasion includes the customary liquor supply. Men expected it at a house raising, but it was also the source of many serious accidents.

Eugene Thwing was born in Quincy, Massachusetts in 1866. Following graduation from Adelphi College in Brooklyn, he embarked on a publishing career. From 1882-1908 he was connected with the publishing firm of Funk and Wagnalls and later published and edited THE CIRCLE AND SUCCESS MAGAZINE. His first book THE RED KEGGERS, was published in 1903. "A burley, brawny, bustling book" set during pioneer days in the Midland areas, it was, according to the BALTIMORE SUN, a "book worth reading; a magnet to draw the interest of even the jaded reader of many novels." Thwing followed up his success with a sequel in 1905, THE MAN

90

The Red Keggers

ROS Whitmore had prospered during the two years since Farmer Hawkins had engaged him to clear the stumps from a section of his farm. He and his good wife Jule were hard workers and missed no opportunity to provide and save for their large and growing brood. The little cabin which they had erected out at The Corners, in the Sturgeon district, when they were among the first pioneers of the region, had long been too small. The time had come at last for building a house more suited to their needs and their position. The Whitmores were popular far and wide among young and old. It was a foregone conclusion that Ros's house-raising bee would eclipse anything of the kind seen in the township.

For weeks Ros had been selecting and bringing from the forest the best long, smooth pine-trees he could find whose diameter at the base was from a foot to fourteen or sixteen inches and tapered to eight or ten inches at a distance of twenty to twenty-four feet from the ground. As he intended to build a good "block" house, he flattened the logs with a broadax, cut them into proper lengths, and squared the ends to make them ready to be placed in their proper position in the house. For the less pretentious houses and for the lumber-shanties the ends of the logs only were squared, and on raising-day the logs were put up with the bark on. Thus they were rather uncouth in appearance, but answered the simple needs of the majority of small farmers. When properly chinked with clay or plaster, these log dwellings were warm and dry in winter, which was a great desideratum. Ros, however, was determined on a very different kind of house. He and his large family had lived long enough in the little rough log cabin of a pioneer. His new house would be one of the finest of its kind within twenty miles, almost as good as that of Farmer Hawkins. All the logs were nicely hewed and squared. The house was to be one and a half stories high, with real sawed rafters, shingles for the roof, siding for the gable ends, and all chinks filled with real lime plaster.

As soon as the logs were cut, trimmed, and ready to be put in place, Ros set a day for the raising, and every able-bodied man within reasonable distance was invited to be present and lend a helping hand. The Saturday following the breaking of the rollway had been selected as a convenient time for the many who had been engaged on the river and had not yet settled down to the regular spring work on their farms.

Raising-bees were always great occasions. The crowd never failed. Drawn by the certainty of a generous spread and plenty to drink, as well as by cordial neighborly feeling, and the unwritten law which governed such events, nearly all who could come did come. The jug was a potent factor. Custom had established it as an indispensable adjunct of every raising-bee, and many young farmers who would have been ashamed to be seen going into Pete's place, partook openly, and often too freely of his "Mystic Brand" at these gatherings, frequently taking their first lessons in dram-drinking. At the wind-up of a raising-bee the sober men were usually a small minority, and often serious accidents befell those whose nerves had been rendered unsteady before the heavy work of the day was finished. Ros was himself a temperate man, and did not approve of the use of liquor, but at a time like this he felt compelled to yield to popular custom and demands. To omit so important an item would be regarded as an unpardonable breach of hospitality, so he provided himself with several jugs of "Pete's best," which, as the latter confidentially informed him, had been specially procured the day before for this occasion. His wife, also, made generous preparations for the great crowd which was sure to be on hand. "Aunt Jule's" dinners were famous for their quality as well as for their quantity, and there were many willing hands to help her, because the women were glad of any excuse to be present as participants in the activity.

Barney had recovered from his bruises sufficiently to attend the raising. Indeed, his presence was regarded as well nigh indispensable, because of his cool head, his ready wit, and his universal popularity. Few, however, were prepared for the announcement made by Sam Hawkins the day before the raising that he also intended to go and help in the work, and that he would do as much as anybody to help Ros Whitmore put up his house.

"As to thet, we'll wait an' see," remarked Tom Moore to Barney, and then he asked, "What idee hes he got in his head, d'ye think? 'Tain't likely he's grown fond o' work all on a sudden."

Barney's eyes flashed, and he clenched his fists, but he merely replied, "Faith, ye'll have to ask me somethin' asier."

On Saturday morning Sam was astir fully two hours earlier than his wont. Both his father and mother marvelled at his unaccustomed activity, but were glad to see it aroused in a good cause. Sam said very little to any one. He was ill-natured and nervous, and seemed to be enlisted in the day's undertaking not because he liked it, but in spite of his dislike of it. Yet no one had urged, or even invited him to attend the raising, taking for granted that it would be useless to do so.

Farmer Hawkins and Mother Hawkins, and Mr. and Mrs. Maloney rode over to Ros Whitmore's immediately after breakfast. Barney and Norine walked there together, while Sam went by himself, and arrived after all the others. Nearly two hundred men, women, and children had gathered on the clearing. Work was about to begin. Two layers of logs were already in place upon the foundation, and others were on the skids waiting to be moved up to form the third tier. The ever-present jug had taken its first round and was about to be placed in the cool shade of a hollow tree near by as Sam sauntered up.

"Seems I'm just in time," he remarked, taking in the situation at a glance. "Pass that jug this way before you set it down. It's good stuff. I can vouch for that, don't you know."

"How's that? What d'ye know about it, more'n anybody else?" asked Arch Fellows, who held the jug, eyeing Sam curiously.

"Oh, you know—that is, I heard Pete say he was going to fetch up from his cellar some of his best stock for this occasion," replied Sam, coloring with sudden embarrassment.

"Reckon ye got thet a leetle mixed, me boy," responded

the other, handing Sam the jug. "Pete told Ros Whitmore es how he'd jes' ordered this lot, special, from his agent for this raisin'. But it's good stuff, es you say, sure enough."

Sam took a deep draught of the liquor.

"Hurry up, Sam!" exclaimed Joe Reon in a half whisper at his side. "Here comes Barney. Ros hes appointed him his assistant superintendent for this job an' asked him to shet off the drinkin' until after the house is up—if he can."

Sam set the jug down with a fierce oath, and seemed on the point of defying Barney then and there, but just beyond Barney he saw the minister talking with Ros Whitmore, and he quickly edged away through the crowd.

"Pile in here, boys," called Barney, whipping off his own coat. "Begorra, this'll be a foine big house, an' we must be after finishin' it before sundown."

Each man was given his place, and the work began in earnest. Five or six tiers were set and made fast without interruption. Then some one started the jug on its rounds again.

"Ye'd better lave the jug alone till the house is up," expostulated Barney; but it was of no use, for the fire had been kindled and the blaze must be kept up. Nobody was content to be left out after some had had their turn, so it was impossible to proceed with the work until all who wished had partaken a second time of Pete's "best."

While the lower tiers were being placed, the work was comparatively easy and safe. The skids rested at a gentle incline, one end on the ground and the other on the highest tier. The heavy logs were moved up this incline by the use of ropes pulled by those above, assisted by the strong arms of those below, who pushed as long as they could reach the rising log. As the walls grew higher and the incline of the skids correspondingly steeper, the work became more difficult, and the element of danger entered. Cool heads, strong arms and backs, and steady nerves were essential. Moreover, the quality of the work depended upon the carefulness used in setting the logs true and fastening the ends securely. Many a house and barn had suffered from neglect in these particulars, caused by too much attention to the jug.

Sam worked gingerly, and skipped from place to place

with apparently no reason, never sticking to any one task more than a few minutes. He was gruff and irritable, and seemed to be dissatisfied with everything. Barney, on the other hand, worked with steady persistence, always at the hardest places, and ready to help wherever there seemed to be any danger of a log slipping. His hearty words of encouragement and exhortation, and his merry laugh and quick wit, inspired all with a greater willingness to work; but he could not persuade them to let the jug alone.

An old lady, a dear old soul, known by all as "Granny," lived in a shanty near by, and although more than eighty years of age, she was possessed of great vigor, and took as much interest in the house-raising as did Ros Whitmore himself. She watched the work from the laying of the first log, and as one by one the tiers went up, and time after time the "Mystic Brand" went around, she began to notice that the corners of the building were showing the effects of too much stimulation on the brain. The condition of "her boys," as she called all the men, worried her greatly, and finally she walked up to a group that had just gathered for another round of drinks and addressed them:

"Look here, boys, don't you think you ought to let me have thet jug for a while? Some of you will surely get hurted. Besides, don't you see what poor work you are doin' on Ros's house? Jes' let me keep it till after dinner, anyhow, and then if you *must* have it I'll give it to you agin."

"Hear what Granny says?" laughed Ned Blakely. "She wants you to give up the jug till arter dinner, an' I guess she's about right."

"I've got er holt o' this jug now, an' don't intend to let go yet," said Jake Vogel, good-humoredly. "But Granny's right, jest the same, an' she can hev it as soon as I get enough," and suiting the action to the word, he took a long "pull" of the stuff. "There," he remarked with a laugh, as he held the jug out to Granny, "I'll be good now. Ye got ter limber up a bit on these neighborly occasions, ye know. I've been ter lots of 'em, an' guess I know when it's time ter stop."

"Jake's a hog," said Tim Underwood, and reaching for the jug before Granny could get it, proceeded to demonstrate that he belonged to the same genus.

Barney and Ros were both getting out of patience, but the good-nature of the crew prevented any outbreak, and as they were all volunteers, extreme measures could not be taken. Even Parson Allen deemed it wise to refrain from remonstrance which would be listened to with perfect good-humor and respect, and then disregarded when his back was turned. Barney was constantly on the alert, and more than once he had sprung to the aid of some half-drunken workman just in time to save him from injury when he got into a dangerous position and had not wit enough to take care of himself. Finally Granny secured the jug, but by that time it was as empty as charity at a charity ball. By the time the noon hour arrived the house was about two-thirds up, and the work was beginning to go better, because one jug was empty and the other had been surreptitiously removed from its hiding-place and smuggled away.

The feast of the day was ready promptly at twelve o'clock, and the hungry men sat down to dinner at a long table made of boards and placed in the shade. White cloths covered the rough pine boards, and great heaps of substantial good things crowded each other from one end to the other. The women and girls bustled about to wait upon the workers, leaving their own repast until later.

Apparently all thought of the jug had been dropped, but as the men returned to the building, on their way a dozen or more of them ranged themselves along in front of Granny's place, and, to this good dame's utter disgust, demanded the article they sought. She argued with them for a while, but seeing argument useless, she finally produced it—empty. There were some who, forgetting that this was just its condition when surrendered to her, accused the dear old soul of dealing unfairly with them. However, Red-Keg being only a few miles distant, a courier was despatched with the jug with orders to lose no time in getting it refilled and back to the place.

The sun was well down in the west when the plates, or finishing logs, were to be put into their places to form the last tier upon which the roof was to rest. In order to raise these heavy logs, longer skids were employed, so that the incline should not be so steep. As before, two ropes were fastened at the top of the building, the lower ends were placed around the log at each end, and men were stationed at the top to pull on the ropes, while others remained below to assist in the lifting as far as they could reach. This dangerous work, which called for clear heads and steady nerves, was undertaken by men some of whom were scarcely able to stand erect upon the ground, so demoralizing had been the effect of the fresh supply of Pete's "Mystic Brand." Only those who had refrained from indulgence realized the gravity of the situation.

When the last log had been lifted and pulled to a point just above the heads of the men below, it was evident that the weight was too great for those above to master, but by a desperate effort they succeeded in pulling it up still farther.

"Boost 'er up, boys! I can't hold on ter this rope much longer!" bawled out Joe Reon at the top.

"Put the rope 'round yer waist," yelled Tim Underwood from below, laughing tipsily; "then ef the log comes down, you'll hev ter come with it. Haw, haw!"

The log dropped back a little till it was again within reach of those on the ground.

"Hurrah, boys, shove 'er up!" shouted Arch Fellows, giving it a boost, and away went that end of the log, while the other end, held above by Sam Hawkins, remained stationary.

This left the log in a most dangerous position, and cool heads were needed to avert a disaster, but the men became dazed, and the danger dawned upon their sodden minds too late.

"My God! boys, what are ye doin' down there?" yelled Joe Reon, who had actually tied the rope around his body as suggested, and was now struggling with all his nerveless strength to prevent the inevitable; "I'm fallin', an' the top log is comin' with me! Look out!"

Barney and Ros, seeing that some one was going to get hurt, both rushed toward the spot where the falling log must strike. Barney was there first, with quick brain and steady nerve taking in the situation at a glance. At the risk of his own life he pushed two men aside who would have been struck by the log in its descent, and then dodging under it, caught the man who was falling just in time to save him from striking his head on a sharp pine stump near by.

Sam, who held the rope at the other end of the log, braced his feet securely and held his end well in place, but just as the shout went up at the daring rescue Barney had made, Sam suddenly let his end go, which, released from duress, slid like lightning down the skid just as Barney was passing under it with Joe Reon still in his arms.

Every one supposed that the log was secure in Sam's hands, and no one had looked for it to fall. But Norine, who had been watching Barney's every movement, had come near to the scene unnoticed, and with quick eye she saw Sam let go of his rope, and almost before the log began to fall she screamed:

"Barney, quick, jump back!"

Without stopping to learn the reason, Barney obeyed his sweetheart's warning instantly, springing backward close to the wall just in time to avoid receiving the whole crushing weight of the log upon his head.

Ros Whitmore was not so fortunate. He had followed close behind Barney at the first sign of the danger. When Barney sprang back, Ros attempted to do the same, but he stumbled and fell to the ground. The heavy log came down upon his right leg and broke the bone below the knee.

Meanwhile, Sam stood above, watching the scene below, but forgot the slack of the rope, which he had gathered in as he had pulled up his end of the log, and which lay in loops and coils about his feet. As the log slid down the skids it jerked the rope with it, and the slack quickly becoming entangled around Sam's feet, pulled him unceremoniously from his position. No one was there to help him. Barney was still holding to Reon, whom he had the instant before caught in his fall. The rest were rushing to help Ros. Sam struggled for a brief moment to release himself from the ropes, and then, with a yell of rage and terror, came tumbling down. A large tub of mortar for filling the chinks between the logs had been started close to the wall just below Sam. The lime had just been slaked, and the sand was ready for mixing. Into this tub Sam fell headlong. The force of the fall was broken, but when Sam emerged from his lime bath he was a sight to behold. Sputtering, and spluttering, and howling, he rushed down to the brook near by and jumped in bodily, and began at once the task of cleaning the stuff out of his eyes and mouth.

A part of the crowd followed, forgetting even Ros's sad injury in this new diversion, and the more Sam raved and swore, the more the spectators laughed and jeered, for Sam was generally disliked by his neighbors, and they did not hesitate to blame him for his own plight. There was no excuse, they said, for his letting go of the rope, if he had had his wits about him, and that was the least that could be said. There were some who said nothing, but shook their heads gravely and turned away.

Barney had taken Joe Reon to Granny's cabin, where he had found the fellow to be more scared than hurt, and then he hastened to look after Ros, stopping on the way to see if Sam had been injured. When he saw the fun the rest were having at Sam's expense he withdrew to Whitmore's cabin, whither Ros had been carried. Already his brave and energetic wife had stripped the injured leg, and, with the help of Mother Hawkins and Parson Allen, was preparing splints and bandages. She knew just what to do, and wasted no time in useless lamentations or complaints.

"It is a very unfortunate interruption of Ros's home-building," said Allen to Barney, quietly; "but we may be thankful it is no worse. He will have the use of his leg again in time with the good care Jule will take of it. She is the best doctor he could have."

Barney said nothing in reply. He did not dare to trust himself, and the sight of little Tilly Whitmore standing by her father's bed and holding his hand tightly in hers while the big tears rolled quietly down her pale, agonized little face, was too much for him altogether. With a choking sensation in his throat, he hurriedly assured Ros that he would see to finishing the house, and that Ros needn't worry, and then broke away from the painful scene and went back to the work outside.

Sam and the rest of the men soon returned, all by this time being pretty well sobered up. Barney looked his enemy in the face as he passed him and saw the demon in the fellow's eyes, but said nothing. Sam was too badly bruised to resume work, and after a short rest

started for home. The jug went around no more that day.

As Barney and Norine walked home together after the work was finished and the sumptuous supper eaten, they were unusually quiet. After walking almost half the distance, Norine, unable longer to keep her dreadful thought to herself, exclaimed:

"Oh, Barney! That's what he came for. He did it on purpose. I saw him——"

"Hush, darlint!" interrupted Barney, who had the same conviction. "Ye can't be sure. Let's not think of it. Let's talk about yer own swate self."

"And imagine," she continued, in only half obedience, "you thought I was going to the dance with him."

"Faith, I'm thinkin' thet was quare meself. But he'll not be there at all, niver fear, an' we kin have our fun better without him, eh, swateheart—thet is, ef we can have any fun at all when we'll be thinkin' of poor Ros lyin' home with a broken leg, an' his little mite of a girl cryin' her swate eyes out for him—all on account of thet—thet—*hellyun!*"

Having thus relieved a part of his pent-up rage through the safety valve of that one expressive word, Barney drew Norine closer to him, and spent the remainder of the time in trying to make her forget everything except himself and happiness.

MY NEW HOME
IN NORTHERN MICHIGAN

LONG after pioneer days had ended in southern Michigan, northern Michigan remained a thinly settled frontier region. Only after the better land had been taken in the south did homesteaders stake out their claims on the less appealing terrain to the north. However, cut over land left by the loggers along the shores of Lake Michigan ultimately proved to be ideal for fruit growing.

Charles W. Jay arrived in the wilderness region of Benona, Oceana County in 1871 to try his hand at fruit farming. The 56 year old editor and public speaker who resembled Horace Greeley in appearance had become disappointed in his career in New Jersey. Northern Michigan beckoned as a place to begin anew. Unfortunately Jay knew nothing about farming. He spent several years clearing his isolated farmstead and planting an orchard, but it never became a successful operation.

Despite his failure as a fruit grower, Jay retained a good sense of humor. He contributed humorous articles to local newspapers under the pen name O.P. Dildock. In 1874 Jay published a facetious account of his experiences as a settler, MY NEW HOME IN NORTHERN MICH— IGAN, AND OTHER TALES. It is a choice example of Michigan humor at its best. Jay remained in Oceana County until his death in 1884. Let us travel back to 1872 and see how a neighbor helped farmer Jay get rid of his potato bugs.

How the "Old Settler" Settled My Potato Bugs

I knew him by his swinging stride and his long rifle, the moment he emerged from the old Indian trail into the clearing.

It was the Old Settler. He came out from Northern Indiana twenty years before, as one of the first lumber camps formed in these wilds by the Chicago Saw Mill Company. He managed, at the end of two years' service in the camps, to get forty acres of land for about the same number of dollars, put up a little log cabn with his own hands, cleared off ten acres, and settled down in contented independence.

The honesty of this Old Settler would bear a heavy discount in any mart outside of Wall street. But there he would be sure of sympathetic and congenial natures. He is a Jay Gould, circumscribed in his genius by lack of material for extended operations. The first spring I came into the settlement, he sold me ten bushels of seed potatoes, at double the market price, every one of which was frozen to the hardest possible solidity. When a week later I discovered this fact, and suggested that he make some sort of reparation, he indignantly remarked:

"Why, stranger, do you take me for a durn'd fool! I'm a poor man. You wear store clothes and keep hosses, and they say hereabouts that you are lousy with greenbacks. But you musn't go for to try to put on style among honest folks here in the woods. Pay you back that money! Not if this individual knows hisself. Who can best afford to lose them 'taters, me or you? When I was up on the Manistee last winter, a loggin', I licked a feller about your size, with one hand tied behind me."

The logic of these remarks would not bear close criticism, but the huge fist which the speaker swung around, in rather careless proximity to my head, by way of emphasis, had a mollifying effect upon my anger. I assured him I was only joking. The Older Settler magnanimously accepted the apology, invited himself to dinner, borrowed three dollars to pay his taxes, and struck out again into the forest. And now he visits me regularly, and in the absence of all neighborly companionship, he is at times rather welcome than otherwise.

When the snows had all melted last Spring, and had poured the last of their tributes into the treasury of the great lake, and the genial days came out from the shadow of the long, fierce winter, I set about my innocent agricultural labors.

Albeit of an indolent organization, and a dreamer rather than a laborer in the great problem of life, still I find myself, in my new mode of existence, compelled to work in self-defense. There is neither store, church, nor tavern, nor any of the accessories of civilization within many miles of my lowly dwelling. The winds sigh mournfully through the forests; day unto day and night unto night speaketh a voiceless language of the past, in the solemn loneliness of these grand old woods. The sounds of labor are few and far between, and seem but the muffled echoes of the general silence.

To avoid the saddening thoughts of death and eternity, which such surroundings force upon the meditations of one accustomed all his life to the remorseless din and struggles of great cities, I went to work like another Abel, who was a tiller of the ground long before the ornamental potato bug was mercifully invented. I prepared an acre for early rose, cut, planted, and covered six bushels theron, and all with these soft hands of mine. The very first forenoon of this work satisfied me that I was the discoverer of a valuable acquisition to medical science. There is some secreted virtue in a Northern Michigan hoe handle, that raises blisters in a few minutes, as large as life, and twice as natural.

Rapacious quack, I have patented the discovery. The subscriber is too smart a Jersey Yankee to make public "a great blessing to mankind," without the preliminary caution of securing the profits.

Well, to make a short story long, my potatoes grew up out of the furrow, drank in the air and the sunshine, and I was happy in the consciousness of rewarded skill and industry. No fond mother ever so watched over the dawning beauty of her first-born, as did your servant, beloved reader, over the developed glory of them 'taters! Alas, for the cruel sequel!

One day

> The bugs they came down, like wolves on the fold,
>
> And eat of my vines all their stomachs could hold!

It was at this fatal juncture that my evil genius, the Old Settler, emerged from the forest, and came upon the scene, as related at the opening of this history. Coming up to where I was sitting moodily upon a stump, feeling like Marias at the ruins of Carthage, only more so, his keen eye took in the situation at once, but his diplomatic caution suggested the disguise of an inquiry:

"What mout the matter be?"

"Look at what was, only yesterday, the most beautiful potato patch in the settlement. In forty-eight hours from this it will be a sandy, herbless waste."

"Bugs, eh?"

"Yes."

"Is that all? Why, stranger, you can kill every blasted critter of 'em, sure as shootin', before 9 o'clock tomorrow mornin'."

In the hour of despondency, the feeblest support gives hope a ray of confidence. I grasped with gratitude the hand of the Old Settler, and eagerly inquired how the work of extermination could be effected.

"Mister," said he, "you're a new beginner, and don't know much about farmin'. But you're a clever feller, as far as *I've* seen, and I'm willin' to give you my 'sperience. Go and get a bushel of fresh lime, what's just outen the kiln. Pound it up as fine as powder, and early in the mornin', when the dew is thick, dust them are vines all over, and by noon there won't be a durn'd live 'tater bug in the hull patch."

With a gush of feeling that uprooted all my previous prejudices, and flushed tearfully in my eyes, I again grasped the hand of the kindly old man, with a mental oath of eternal friendship; hitched up "Prince," and drove like Jehu, the son of none, to Stony Creek, eight miles distant; got back at dusk with the lime, and worked and sweated all night in reducing it to powder. I stole out exultingly in the early grey of the morning, and gave a magnificent dusting to the whole patch!

My triumph was of the kind supposed to be loved by the gods, for it died young. Even as I waited and watched, the dust began to seethe and bubble, and a smoke steamed up, and the vines squirmed, and writhed, and soon lay prone upon the ground!

"Fine arternoon," exclaimed the Old Settler, as he strode into the patch where I was contemplating the ruins.

I looked in the man's face sternly for a full minute, expecting to see him quail in the consciousness of guilt, in full sight of the injury he had done me. But the steel blue of his eye remained unclouded with shame, as he observed, in a satisfied tone:

"Well, stranger, you see the lime has cleared the kitchen. Bugs all dead, I b'lieve?"

"Yes," I bitterly rejoined, "and *vines,* too. Did you know it would kill the vines?"

"Why, of *course* I know'd it would kill the 'taters. Any durn'd fool, who had the sense he was born with, oughter to know *that!* But then *look at the satisfaction of carcumwentin' the cussed bugs!"*

I here tightened my grasp upon the hoe handle, set my teeth hard, and breathed determinedly. But a spirit of Christian forbearance came in time to save me from the contemplated violence. I thought of the feller he had licked up on the Manistee, and grinned horribly a ghastly smile as I lifted my eight-dollar beaver from my head, and handed it to the Old Settler with a bow, and the exclamation of—

"Take my hat!"

To my surprise and consternation, the matter-of-fact nature of my tormenter seemed to take the offer as of good faith, and as a reward for acceptable service rendered! He stretched forth his long muscular arm, and before I could withdraw the offer, he had it safely in hand. He then lifted his own rimless, greasy, dilapidated "slouch" from his head, tucked it under his arm, put my "pride of New York" on his shaggy nob, and looked happy. He soon took it off, examined with pride and satisfaction the beautiful finish of the interior, replaced it upon his head, and spoke thus:

"Thank you, mister. This is the fust present I've had this many a year. Some of the folks here in the woods think you are a man of too big feelin' for sich as us. I've always found you to be a clever feller, without a bit of the gentleman about you, and I'll stand up for you while there's a hemlock tree on Point Sable, or a ten-pound pickerel in Bear Lake."

Thus leaving his sense of gratitude to console me in his absence, the Old Settler struck out toward the forest, in the direction of his cabin. On reaching the top of the hill, he halted for a moment, again removed *my* new hat, again scrutinized the beautiful interior, smoothed the body affectionately with his coat sleeve, replaced it, and was soon lost to sight, and not particularly dear to memory.

THE BLAZED TRAIL

FEW aspects of Michigan's past have so captured the popular imagination as the colorful heyday of the lumbermen. Tales of the rough and tumble days when men were men have fascinated generations of readers. Shanty boys and river hogs, Paul Bunyan and Silver Jack Driscoll, cross cut saws and cant hooks, log slides and river drives have become part of American popular culture.

The harvesting, sawing and marketing of white pine dominated the state's economy from the Civil War to the turn of the century. Timber barons made fortunes, thousands of lumberjacks found employment, and Michigan wood built Chicago twice. The large scale exploitation of timber began in the dense pine forests of the Saginaw County. More than 3 million acres of virgin white pine lay along a network of streams that fed the Saginaw River. By 1854 the 29 mills in the Saginaw Valley had a capacity of 100 million board feet per year.

The Cass River region of the Saginaw Valley became the setting for Stewart Edward White's novel about the logging industry, THE BLAZED TRAIL. White was born in Grand Rapids in 1873 and spent his first nine years in a small northern lumber mill town. Following graduation from Grand Rapids High School and the University of Michigan in 1895, he spent several years adventuring on the Great Lakes and out west. White wrote THE BLAZED TRAIL in the Hudson's Bay country one snow bound winter. He based it on stories related by his father, a lumberman.

The novel was published in 1902 and quickly established White's reputation as an adventure writer. *THE BLAZED TRAIL* became a best seller and remained in print for more than thirty years. White's other works about Michigan lumbering include *BLAZED TRAIL STORIES (1904)*, *THE RIVER MAN (1908)* and *THE ADVENTURES OF BOBBY ORDE (1911)*. His bibliography eventually encompassed over forty volumes of fiction, travel, hunting, biography, and spiritualism.

The Blazed Trail

AS soon as loading began, the cook served breakfast at three o'clock. The men worked by the light of torches, which were often merely catsup jugs with wicking in the necks. Nothing could be more picturesque than a teamster conducting one of his great pyramidical loads over the little inequalities of the road, in the ticklish places standing atop with the bent knee of the Roman charioteer, spying and forestalling the chances of the way with a fixed eye and an intense concentration that relaxed not one inch in the miles of the haul. Thorpe had become a full-fledged cant-hook man.

He liked the work. There is about it a skill that fascinates. A man grips suddenly with the hook of his strong instrument, stopping one end that the other may slide; he thrusts the short, strong stock between the log and the skid, allowing it to be overrun; he stops the roll with a sudden sure grasp applied at just the right moment to be effective. Sometimes he allows himself to be carried up bodily, clinging to the cant-hook like an acrobat to a bar, until the log has rolled once; when, his weapon loosened, he drops lightly, easily to the ground. And it is exciting to pile the logs on the sleigh, first a layer of five, say; then one of six smaller; of but three; of two; until, at the very apex, the last is dragged slowly up the skids, poised, and, just as it is about to plunge down the other side, is gripped and held inexorably by the little men in blue flannel shirts.

Chains bind the loads. And if ever, during the loading, or afterwards when the sleigh is in motion, the weight of the logs causes the pyramid to break down and squash out; — then woe to the driver, or whoever happens to be near! A saw log does not make a great deal of fuss while falling, but it falls through anything that happens in its way, and a man who gets mixed up in a load of twenty-five or thirty of them obeying the laws of gravitation from a height of some fifteen to twenty feet, can be crushed into strange shapes and fragments. For this reason the loaders are picked and careful men.

At the banking grounds, which lie in and about the bed of the river, the logs are piled in a gigantic skidway to a-wait the spring freshets, which will carry them down stream to the "boom." In that enclosure they remain until sawed in the mill.

Such is the drama of the saw log, a story of grit, resourcefulness, adaptability, fortitude and ingenuity hard to match. Conditions never repeat themselves in the woods as they do in the factory. The wilderness offers ever new complications to solve, difficulties to overcome. A man must think of everything, figure on everything, from the grand sweep of the country at large to the pressure on a king-bolt. And where another possesses the boundless resources of a great city, he has to rely on the material stored in one corner of a shed. It is easy to build a palace with men and tools; it is difficult to build a log cabin with nothing but an ax. His wits must help him where his experience fails; and his experience must push him mechanically along the track of habit when successive buffetings have beaten his wits out of his head. In a day he must construct elaborate engines, roads, and implements which old civilization considers the works of leisure. Without a thought of expense he must abandon as temporary, property which other industries cry out at being compelled to acquire as permanent. For this reason he becomes in time different from his fellows. The wilderness leaves something of her mystery in his eyes, that mystery of hidden, unknown but guessed, power. Men look after him on the street, as they would look after any other pioneer, in vague admiration of a scope more virile than their own.

Thorpe, in common with the other men, had thought Radway's vacation at Christmas time a mistake. He could not but admire the feverish animation that now characterized the jobber. Every mischance was as quickly repaired as aroused expedient could do the work.

The marsh received first attention. There the restless

snow drifted uneasily before the wind. Nearly every day the road had to be plowed, and the sprinklers followed the teams almost constantly. Often it was bitter cold, but no one dared to suggest to the determined jobber that it might be better to remain indoors. The men knew as well as he that the heavy February snows would block traffic beyond hope of extrication.

As it was, several times an especially heavy fall clogged the way. The snow-plow, even with extra teams, could hardly force its path through. Men with shovels helped. Often but a few loads a day, and they small, could be forced to the banks by the utmost exertions of the entire crew. *Esprit de corps* awoke. The men sprang to their tasks with alacrity, gave more than an hour's exertion to each of the twenty-four, took a pride in repulsing the assaults of the great enemy, whom they personified under the generic "She." Mike McGovern raked up a saint somewhere whom he apostrophized in a personal and familiar manner.

He hit his head against an overhanging branch.

"You're a nice wan, now ain't ye?" he cried angrily at the unfortunate guardian of his soul. "Dom if Oi don't quit ye! Ye see!"

"Be the gate of Hivin!" he shouted, when he opened the door of mornings and discovered another six inches of snow, "Ye're a burrd! If Oi couldn't make out to be more of a saint than that, Oi'd quit the biznis! Move yor pull, an' get us some dacint weather! Ye awt t' be road monkeyin' on th' golden streets, thot's what ye awt to be doin'!"

Jackson Hines was righteously indignant, but with the shrewdness of the old man, put the blame partly where it belonged.

"I ain't sayin'," he observed judicially, "that this weather ain't hell. It's hell and repeat. But a man sort've got to expec' weather. He looks for it, and he oughta be ready for it. The trouble is we got behind Christmas. It's that Dyer. He's about as mean as they make 'em. The only reason he didn't die long ago is becuz th' Devil's thought him too mean to pay any 'tention to. If ever he should die an' go to Heaven he'd pry up th' golden streets an' use the infernal pit for a smelter."

With this magnificent bit of invective, Jackson seized a lantern and stumped out to see that the teamsters fed their horses properly.

"Didn't know you were a miner, Jackson," called Thorpe, laughing.

"Young feller," replied Jackson at the door, "it's a lot easier to tell what I *ain't* been."

So floundering, battling, making a little progress every day, the strife continued.

One morning in February, Thorpe was helping load a big butt log. He was engaged in "sending up"; that is, he was one of the two men who stand at either side of the skids to help the ascending log keep straight and true to its bed on the pile. His assistant's end caught on a sliver, ground for a second, and slipped back. Thus the log ran slanting across the skids instead of perpendicular to them. To rectify the fault, Thorpe dug his cant-hook into the timber and threw his weight on the stock. He hoped in this manner to check correspondingly the ascent of his end. In other words, he took the place, on his side, of the preventing sliver, so equalizing the pressure and forcing the timber to its proper position. Instead of rolling, the log slid. The stock of the cant-hook was jerked from his hands. He fell back, and the cant-hook, after clinging for a moment to the rough bark, snapped down and hit him a crushing blow on the top of the head.

Had a less experienced man than Jim Gladys been stationed at the other end, Thorpe's life would have ended there. A shout of surprise or horror would have stopped the horse pulling on the decking chain; the heavy stick would have slid back on the prostrate young man, who would have thereupon been ground to atoms as he lay. With the utmost coolness Gladys swarmed the slanting face of the load; interposed the length of his cant-hook stock between the log and it; held it exactly long enough to straighten the timber, but not so long as to crush his own head and arm; and ducked, just as the great piece of wood rumbled over the end of the skids and dropped with a thud into the place Norton, the "top" man, had prepared for it.

It was a fine deed, quickly thought, quickly dared. No one saw it. Jim Gladys was a hero, but a hero without an audience.

They took Thorpe up and carried him in, just as they had carried Hank Paul before. Men who had not spoken a dozen words to him in as many days gathered his few belongings and stuffed them awkwardly into his satchel. Jackson Hines prepared the bed of straw and warm blankets in the bottom of the sleigh that was to take him out.

"He would have made a good boss," said the old fellow. "He's a hard man to nick."

Thorpe was carried in from the front, and the battle went on without him.

TIMBER

GIANT stands of white pine grew on Michigan's sandy soil. Lumberjacks left only stumps, barren waste lands ravished by seasonal forest fires. Unscrupulous real estate agents duped would be farmers to return to this sterile land. Their holdings were soon up for tax sale. As Michigan's timber resources, once thought limitless, grew increasingly scarce, the novel theory of reforestation presented an alternative to unproductive cut over land.

Harold Titus based his novel, TIMBER, about one such reforestation attempt in northern Michigan. The plot concerns the efforts of a young women to hold onto the white pine forest her father had planted half a century before. A rich old lumber baron, a dishonest lawyer and other jealous adversaries seek to rob her of her property. When all other efforts fail, an intentionally set forest fire threatens to destroy everything in its path.

Harold Titus was born and raised in the Grand Traverse region. He graduated from the University of Michigan in 1911, worked as a police reporter for the DETROIT NEWS and served in the army during World War I. Following the war, he returned to Traverse City where he operated a fruit farm and further developed his craft of writing fiction. He turned out hundreds of adventure stories for popular magazines. TIMBER, published in 1922, was Titus's first novel with a Michigan setting.

Following a trout fishing trip to an old camping spot that had been "devastated by pulp wood scavengers and ravaged by fire", Titus wrote TIMBER to promote an alternative use of the cut over lands. It went through several editions during the 1920's, and a silent movie version appeared as *HEARTS AFLAME*. *Titus wrote other Michigan novels including THE BELOVED PAWN (1923), set on Beaver Island, SPINDRIFT (1925), about the Lake Michigan fishing industry and BLACK FEATHER (1936), a historical novel about the Mackinac Island fur trade. TIMBER offers an exciting plot, a love story and realistic descriptions of northern Michigan in the 1920's.*

Timber

BOBBY KILDARE ran shrieking across the dooryard to the big bell and began ringing furiously. In the garage Joe and the cook lowered the platform of fire extinguishers to the car and clamped it fast. Helen was on the driver's seat, waiting for Aunty May who hurried toward her.

" 'Phone Raymer at the mill to turn out everybody. Keep Bobby ringing and Milt will hear the bell. Tell him to send all men to me on lot eighteen—eighteen—south of old cranberry marsh. Remember that: Eighteen, south of the marsh." She spoke slowly and very distinctly.

"Have Milt get Sim Burns on the wire and make him come here with men. Threaten him if he tries to lie down. You stay by the telephone when he is through and get Humphrey Bryant and have him send help from Pancake, if we send word to you we need it.

"All ready, Joe?"

"Let her go!"

The motor spun; the exhaust roared in the small building; the car shot forward and careening drunkenly rounded the house, throwing sand from the ruts and rocking the chemical tanks on its platform. With throttle open to the last notch the girl, heart racing with her motor, tore into the murk, the smell of burning pine growing strong in her nostrils. They crossed the pole bridge that spanned the river with a bouncing and a terrific clatter, due west, then north, slowing on the turns, into denser smoke with each rod traveled; to the westward again and Helen fancied she could feel the heat of burning wood in her face.

"There she is!" cried Joe.

The brakes set and the car stopped in twice its length. They were on the ground in an instant. Beauchamp and Joe tugging at the chemical tanks, running forward along the north-and-south fire line and then plunging into the forest to meet the advancing flames. A muffled shouting behind them; a thwacking of a stick on flesh, and a patrolman galloped up, bringing his apparatus.

"Get in there, Thatcher," Helen said shortly. "There are three others. Take two tanks."

A brass cylinder in either hand the man sped away, the girl behind him. The flames had started from the western boundary of the forest and on this fire line, a half mile in, they could feel their heat, could hear the snap and crackle. The smoke smarted the girl's eyes as she ran forward; it bit her throat and lungs and nostrils.

The forest was a weird company of indistinct tree trunks, the nearest swathed in flowing smoke, those a rod away barely distinguishable. A figure moved before Helen, crouched, going slowly toward the north: Black Joe his tank upended and nozzle playing on the angry tongues of red flame licking along the ground, feeding on dead needles and duff, going swiftly up the stems of small brush, leaping here and there for a hold on a tree trunk, falling back, trying again—the spit of the chemical blotted tongues out, the duff yielded dense smoke instead of flame, the fire sputtered angrily as it was torn loose from its hold on firm wood—

She moved beside Black Joe without speaking, straining her eyes, listening. She heard a shout from beyond and a voice lifted in quick answer. The tank sputtered and went dead. Joe ran back and came with the other fresh one he had brought from the car; but before it could go into play the flames that he had beaten down had found hold again. Their roots were deep in that pitchy duff and he was forced to fight a second time for ground he had already won.

The girl left him and went on. The fire was advancing from west to east, spreading north and south in a fan-shaped area as the wind drove it on. She passed Beauchamp, who coughed as he told her that he, too, had emptied a tank and was covering the same ground for a second time. She came on the patrolman who had reported the fire.

All along she could see those hungry, reaching tongues. One had found hold on a dead branch six feet up a tree and was waxing stalwart on the secreted pitch. She seized a stick and beat it out, shielding her face from the heat with the other arm—and ran on, to see flames crawling up other trees, like nimble devils.

She heard a horse snorting loudly as he came near with a cart of tanks and, a working idea of the size and progress of the fire in her mind, she stumbled back to join the fighters who gathered about.

"Joe, Thatcher, Beauchamp; you handle the chemicals. I'll refill. You," to the other patrolman, "bring in the empties and take out live ones. Make every pint count. It's hot and running fast."

As she tore the lid from the cask of soda and opened the water keg, she planned her battle; three men to fight, one man to carry. A tank was not good for more than a hundred feet of fire front in this heat. Three hundred feet—She shook her head. She needed help!

Another patrolman brought his lathered horse to a stop.

"It's all in this block," Helen said, without stopping her work. "Take your apparatus straight ahead. You'll stay in this east-and-west line. The fire will be north of you and your job is to keep this flank from crossing the line. You'll have help as soon as I can spare men."

The man yelled at his horse. The frightened animal was trying to back and turn and had no terror of the whip. Helen seized the bridle and led him forward, then sprang aside as he lurched on. Her helper emerged. His eyebrows were gone, she saw. He peered close into her face, fright stamped on his features and stared so a moment before he gasped:

"They can't hold it. Soon's they get it knocked down— the wind—the wind throws her along again."

The crackle and pop of burning wood was louder, nearer, the heat more intense, smoke thicker—greenish, yellow smoke, coming in puffs that spread about her and swirled and clung to the ground and then shot upward— or rolled along among the trees.

Black Joe came on a run.

"It's hotter 'n th' hubs of hell! It'll go into the tops if we don't kill it—and up there once, she'll go clear to th' river!"

"I know, Joe. Listen!" From afar off a feeble, thin cry came through the confusion of heavier sounds: the wail of an automobile siren.

It rose and fell, approached and receded in the face of fire sounds, but it was constant and seemed to be shrieking a warning in words: "Git outta the way! We're a-comin'—we're a-comin'—we couldn't stop if we wanted to—we're a-comin'—a-comin'—*now!*"

"That's Raymer and help!" the girl cried and laughed excitedly.

They came clanking through the smoke, Raymer and Goddard, Thad Parker and four others from the mill. They clustered about the girl, but before they could question, she was giving orders. One by one she assigned them to their work. Goddard with a crew to backfire from the next fire line eastward, Black Joe to go on a horse and circle the entire burning area. Raymer to the northern flank. They scattered and Helen, relieved of actual labor, turned her car about and drove back a half mile to a vantage point.

The snapping became sharp reports, like pistol shots. A freakish wind, set up by the rising heat, eddied about, slapping downward and up, this way and that, scattering brands as it went. For a moment a strange silence, then the popping again. Along the line of advancing fire the men worked, shirts smoking as they paved their chemicals. Their hair singed, their cheeks blistered; lungs became raw and eyes streamed water. They retreated slowly, always retreated. They could not advance, could not even make a stand. Checked here, the fire found an opening there and worked into fresh fuel; subdued in this place, it gathered strength elsewhere, and all the time it became more aspiring, leaping higher on trunks, clinging longer to dead branches, running up the lichen-covered bark, licking for the green needles, falling back, waiting, gathering strength and trying again. On the flanks the advance of flame was slower, the heat not so great, the smoke not so dense. They could hold the fire from progress there— But that center kept on relentlessly!

From the tool cache Goddard brought his equipment and men ran along the first fire line to the eastward of the blaze, igniting the duff and brush until forty rods of fire worked backward against the wind slowly to meet the fire which came on toward it. Men paced the fire line, holding their tortured eyes open to watch for brands that might cross the strip and fall into the timber on the far side to start new fires. To combat this menace they carried wet sacks.

Another car arrived, driven by the clerk of Lincoln township, bringing more aid; men ran to the work on Helen's orders and the car drove off to summon others.

Black Joe came up on a panting horse. He slid to the ground and lifted his red, red eyes to the girl who stood in her car and gasped:

"It's a 'bug' fire! Somebody's set this on us!"

"*Set* it?"

"It didn't come in from outside, Helen. Somebody drug a lot of dry bresh in offen that hardwood clearin'. One man, by his tracks—must've worked all night. He tetched it off twenty rod from th' outside fire line— That's what made her hot from th' start!"

The girl fought down her rising rage. To yield to such emotion now would play into the hands of this incendiary. She must think of no yesterday, no tomorrow; she must think of one thing: this fire; on time, this hour!—

"Forget that, Joe! We'll get him later. Side lines going to hold? Back fire all right? Milt there? Where's the front of it now?"

He answered her briefly and mounted again but swung his horse back beside the car.

"If it crosses here," indicating the line where the back fire had started—"you've got Burned Dog swale to fight!"

"I know that, Joe—and we can't *let* it cross!"

"I wasn't tryin' to learn you nothin'," he said apologetically, searching her set face.

Centuries ago when glaciers gouged out this Blueberry country the ridges were laid in strange patterns. Burned Dog Creek, a very small stream, drained a thin ribbon of swamp in the depth of the pine. It ran nearly due east until, meeting the abutment of a ridge that lay between it and the river, it swung sharply to the northward. But from the face of bluff springs seeped and for two-thirds of the way to its pine-crested top the balsam, which lined the creek, grew— If fire should go down that swale, igniting the balsams it would run rapidly, it would shoot up the inflammable cover of that bluff and mount the ridge with a hold in the pine tops that could not be denied; and then it could sweep on to the river, perhaps even across the Blueberry itself, destroying utterly as it went.

If Goddard's back-fire should fail! They could make one more stand, true, but that next line of defense dipped through the first of the balsam itself and if living flame got that far their fighting this morning would have been in vain!

The draft of the conflagration sucked at the back-fire. It moved faster, burning clean as it went, its flame tendrils and smoke banners drawn against the wind by the increasing draft. The crackling had grown to a heavy mutter. The two ragged lines of flame drew nearer. At a hundred yards apart each moved as fast as a man would saunter; at half that distance they reached for one another, fluttering, sweeping across the intervening space, gathering both speed and height. A dull, increasing roar of ascending air sounded beneath the pistol-like reports of burning wood; the yellowish, thick smoke rose as it might through a heated flue—Flame touched flame at the extreme point and that contact seemed to give the strength which swept the laggard portions of the lines forward even faster. A tongue of flame found hold in a pitch deposit on the side of a tree; the draft swept it upward, giving it hold, made it secure there. A long creeper of live fire whipped into the branches dragging heavier flame with it—There was a sound like a great, savage sigh of triumph and a sheet of fire rose from earth crowns and with a ripping, tearing, wailing fury of sound the tops burst into flame—

Trees rocked and twisted in the force of the draft. A mighty column of smoke spouted into the heavens, rising straight up, seeming uninfluenced by the wind and from it rained needles and twigs and small branches, all blazing, and from it came sounds of terror, sounds that went straight through the reason of strong men and touched raw emotions that had been buried for generations. Fire, man's first friend, had turned into his raging enemy, mighty in its wrath, terrible in its manifestation of power.

Men dropped their tools and ran. Goddard raised his

hoarse voice in command to call them back, but he could not be heard—they fled, scattering as the fire leaped the break and fastened itself in the tops of the trees they had sought to safeguard! Thad Parker ran down the line and would have gone on into the forest, heedless of all else except the impulse to escape this fiend, but Helen Foraker caught him by the wrist and swung him about to face her.

"Stay here!" she cried, and shook him. "I need you. There's no danger to you and we've got to try again!—Won't you stay?" to another man, "And you? I need you!"

Others came up, singed, shaken men and assembled about the car as Helen started her motor. They recovered some of their balance when they saw that she was not afraid.

"Get aboard, all of you!" she cried and they scrambled up eagerly, for she was headed away from the monster that raged eighty rods from them—

She drove through the smoke, stopping at another tool cache, swinging into the next fire line, half a mile to the eastward. The men ran forward after Goddard, axes and saws and shovels ready for the new attempt. The fire which had leaped upward and swept onward with such initial savagery, hesitated when it entered the trees that stood above cool ground. No draft held it aloft there and a mighty draft dragged from behind. A puff of cooler air slapped downward, driving a point of the fire from the top in which it burned to the ground. It found hold in the duff about the trunk— The crowns about it burned out, the fire dribbled to the dead needles again. Once more men had their chance. The fire was again a ground fire, no longer breaking through the canopy of tops!

Along the new line of defense trees fell, tops into the forest. Axe and saw slashed and bit, leveling the outer rows to make the break from canopy to canopy wider— And to the windward of these axemen others again started fire to burn out and meet and check fire.

Burned Dog tumbled through the pine here and just before it reached the fire line its current slowed as it settled into the head of the swale, and the pine gave up to balsam and spruce.

Men worked like mad. Goddard drove them, tense and ruthless. Once a man hesitated and Milt struck him heavily, knocking him down, kicking him toward the work he had indicated. None noticed. The man got to his feet and went at the task, the frightful sound of advancing fire neutralizing his resentment. Black Joe was there, barking the oaths of rivermen as he drove the others into the work. The hot wind, rushing down the creek, bobbed the stiff balsams, lifted their branches up to expose the pitch blisters—The nodding, the beckoning of those trees, seemed to invite the visitation which would be their death.

Back in the face of the advancing flame where the chemicals had again been tried, men gave up. Human flesh and will could not stand before that blast. Unhampered, the flames leaped higher, ran faster before the wind, spread their front wider and their growing draft again picked up brands and flung them out over the heads of those who worked feverishly. Islands of fire appeared ahead of the main front. Smoke ascended from a dozen fresh points and men ran from place to place beating them out, but their strategy was disorganized, their forces scattered, efficiency lost.

"All hell can't stop it!" shouted Black Joe as he came up to Helen Foraker, who was dispatching fresh arrivals to relieve worn men. "It'll hit that balsam and go down the creek to the bluff. It'll go up that like an explosion!"

He started away. His last words echoed in the girl's consciousness, hammering at some hidden idea—

Explosion!—"Black Joe!" her voice was shrill and he wheeled. "If it goes up like an explosion, can't an explosion stop it?"

"Huh? What's—"

"Dynamite, Joe! Dynamite!"

"Oh, God help you, Miss Helen! God help you," he cried, with a new excitement, the stimulus of a fresh hope in his voice.

A car was there, its owner begging for an errand. He had brought men from Pancake, men who had scorned and scoffed at Foraker's Folly, but fire closes breaches, belittles differences and those he brought were now at work; this man awaited the girl's word.

"Take Joe!" she said to him. "Push him, Joe!"

The man sprang into his seat, glad to obey her orders. Across the pole bridge they tore, past the big house, on to a dugout in the river bank. Boxes of dynamite were tossed into the car, a coil of fine wire thrown in and, holding a box of percussion caps high, Joe swore as he ordered the other to drive back.

Helen left her post for she could do no good there. Men were wearing out, they were deserting sneaking away under cover of the smoke and she kept among those who remained, a soaked handkerchief over her mouth. The roar of the oncoming fire increased; it commenced to mutter again and the back-fire, feeling the pull of that hot draft, leaped and ate toward its kind—

A sucking sound, a flapping, like an immense flag in a heavy puff of wind, a long-drawn *wo-o-o-sh*, and a great eddy of fire and smoke was sucked upward and scattered. It left the tops through which it had passed only singed but the brands it had lifted were snatched by the gale and swept along, falling, a thousand of them, into the balsam thicket!

A crackling followed, like a growing, harsh laugh. A million matches scratching; a thousand bull whips popping—A ripping, a tearing—The swale was afire and the flame, bursting from great puffs of thick, greenish smoke, exploding, leaping, swept on down the creek, melting all that stood in its path!

"Get Raymer!" Helen shouted, mouth close to Goddard's ear. "Send him to the top of the bluff—and come yourself—"

Again she sped with her car through the smoke, reckless of others who might be in her path. She went up a rising road, hot ashes falling about her and stopped, leaping out, calling aloud to Black Joe.

As well have whispered! From the crest of the ridge she looked down through the smoke-screened balsams sixty feet below to see the inferno beyond, sending up its torrent of triumphant sounds: the rip and tear of flame banners frazzled out by their own heat, the popping, the snapping, now and again a sound like a gun-shot; a mighty, breathy wailing—and all against the background of savage roar!

Joe was on his knees, driving his crow bar into the brink of the bluff. A half-dozen others were doing likewise, making parallel rows of holes among the roots of those pines that grew above the ladder of balsam tips on which that fire would mount.

Others took up the work and Joe, relieved, ran back to tear open the boxes of powder. His hands trembled and he had no ear for Helen. Now and then he glanced into that furnace blast from below and his lips moved soundlessly—Goddard joined him.

Thad Parker ran up, gibbering, an axe in his hands.

"It'll burn us all!" he screamed. "We can't get out!"

Some one grasped and shook him, but Thad would not listen. His eyes were those of a mad man and the cries that came from his throat grew inarticulate. He bit at the man who held him, tried to lift the axe and swing it at his captor. The other staggered away and Thad turned and fled into the smoke—

Joe and Milt fitted caps to the dynamite and Raymer came up on a gasping horse. He caught the idea at a word from Helen and began setting wires. It was delicate work, painful work under those conditions. Time sped!

The cars were backed out and down the grade, but Helen gave no heed. She followed closely the men who were making this, her last big play. The greasy sticks went into the ground, one by one, tamped carefully in their holes along the brink. For two hundred yards they were planted and when the last cap was being adjusted the furnace blast from below tore at the crowns of the pine trees above them with the strength of a tornado.

The girl was atremble as she settled herself beside Joe and the coil box behind a tree trunk, prostrate on the ground, screening her face with her hands from the heat. She could not speak, could not think, could hear nothing but that crescendoing roar from below. Black Joe crouched on his knees, skin blistering through his shirt, peered over the brink. He saw a streamer of flame leap upward through the broiling heat waves, wrenching at balsams as it seared them, saw another fork stab out, saw a solid wall of fire flutter and hesitate and then wrap about the topmost balsams, clinging there a split instant before it made its last leap—its leap into the pine above.

Through that bedlam of terror, Helen's voice cut like a knife: *"Now Joe!"*

She was thrown from her knees to her face because as that sheet of flame gathered itself for its jump into the pine tops, the whole bluff belched out to meet it! A thousand tons of loose sand were flung into the face of the fire. Outward and up and down, it struck, more vicious than the heat in its path, more powerful than the flame. Trees on the brink rocked as the root holds that had endured throughout their life gave way. They swayed and twisted and three, one after the other, toppled over into that smoking maw!—

Smoking maw! The flame was gone. As a puff of breath will extinguish a candle, so that blast had blown life from the fire. For yards, the balsam that had blazed was smothered with dry sand. For rods, the fire was stripped clean from wood where it had found hold. The point of the fire was broken, gone. It was no longer in the balsam tops, no longer a menace to the pine above. It had consumed as it went; there was nothing left in the path of that which had escaped the full force of the explosion to feed upon. It would burn for days, perhaps, but it was down there, disorganized, where men could seize upon and fight it!

"Oh, God A'mighty!" cried Black Joe. "If Paul Bunion could 'a' saw that!"

"Herd back that crew!" choked Helen. "We can hold it, now!"

WHERE COPPER WAS KING

COPPER, a natural resource rivaling timber in value, had become an important aspect of Michigan's economy by the 1860's. The early French explorers knew of upper peninsula copper lodes, and Henry Schoolcraft mentioned copper deposits in the 1820's. But when first state geologist Douglas Houghton reported the extensive copper deposits along the southern Lake Superior shore, he triggered a copper rush to the Keweenaw Peninsula in 1843.

The Cliff Mine near Eagle River became the first successful venture by New England capitalists. When the Sault Locks opened in 1855 and made transportation of copper practical, many other mines in the Keweenaw Peninsula and Ontonagon area went into operation. The Minnesota, Quincy and Calumet and Hecla became famous mines. The immigrants from Finland and Cornwall who arrived to work the mines made a major contribution to the ethnic character of much of the upper peninsula.

James North Wright provided a picture of life during the early Copper mining days on Lake Superior. Wright, a native of Connecticut, first came to the upper peninsula in 1859, at the age of 20. His first job was clerk at the Minnesota Mine. He transferred to the Quincy Mine where he worked his way up to become agent. In 1872 Wright took over as General Superintendent of the Calumet and Hecla Mine. Upon retiring Wright drew upon his experiences of over forty years in the copper country to write the novel WHEN COPPER WAS KING in 1905.

An Underground Incident

HAYDEN soon became acquainted with the officers and their assistants at the mine, — a task easy of accomplishment, as they numbered not more than two score in all. He also rapidly became familiar with his duties at the draughting-room. He was a thorough student, and although he lacked experience in the profession he had chosen, his training had been so good, that, by the aid of exceptionally quick perceptive powers, he easily mastered the work assigned him, and did it well. He had not yet been sent underground, and he waited with some impatience for the time to come when he should be allowed to take up that portion of the work, which he had looked forward to with greatest interest.

One evening, as they were leaving the office, Captain Eastman said to him that some "levels" were to be given for a party of miners drifting in the bottom of the mine, and that in the morning he would like to have him go down with Mr. Edmunds, his first assistant, and do the work. Hayden was delighted with the prospect, and promised to be early at the "changing-house"· on the morrow. That he might cause no delay, he was there a half-hour before the whistle blew for seven o'clock, and was obliged to wait a whole hour for Edmunds, who was often behind time in getting to his work.

Edmunds, or "Lute," as he was familiarly called, was a character who merits description. As he was now seen by Hayden, hurriedly approaching the changing-house, he resembled more an Indian or half-breed than a white man. He was tall and lank, and walked with a quick, nervous stride, his toes turned in, or pointing straight before him, as though he were accustomed to keeping a narrow trail. His face was thin, his skin brown, and tanned by the sun and wind until it resembled parchment. His eyes were small, but dark and piercing. His beard was long and never trimmed, and his long black hair, pushed behind ears, hung down over his neck. He stooped as he walked, and rarely raised his eyes from the ground.

For dress he cared nothing; and his life, which had most of it been spent on the frontier and in the forests, had made him so utterly negligent of everything of the sort, that it was with the greatest difficulty that he was persuaded to clothe himself to meet the changing seasons with decency and comfort. His favorite foot-gear was "German" socks and moccasins. He put on the latter early in the fall, and wore them until the melting snows compelled him to lay them aside in the spring. Then he put on rubber overshoes over his socks, and wore them all summer.

He was an inveterate smoker, and his pipe was never out of his mouth except when necessity compelled it.

His professional knowledge was good, but his habits were so careless and slovenly, that his work was apt to be inaccurate and faulty; and Captain Eastman usually examined his computations before allowing them to be recorded.

Edmunds was an incessant reader, and, in this way, had acquired a large stock of general knowledge. He interested Hayden, who was much amused by his eccentricities, and surprised at the accuracy of his memory and his fund of information on many subjects. He was friendly and sociable, always ready to talk, and fond of discussion; so that they had already become pretty well acquainted.

Just behind Edmunds followed a stout, dull-faced Finn, with the tripod thrown across his shoulder, and the instrument under his arm. Lute looked around just in time to see him slip on the muddy path, and nearly fall to the ground. He called to him sharply:

"Look out there, you stupid blockhead, don't you drop that instrument into the mud."

Then he asked Hayden if he had been there long, and, without waiting for an answer, said: "I was a little late myself, but this damned Finlander misunderstood the captain's orders last night, and had already gone underground, and I had to get him up again, and send him back to the office for my instruments."

They went into the changing-house, and proceeded to put on their underground attire. When all were ready, and Hayden found himself for the first time arrayed in woolen shirt, duck suit, hobnailed boots, and hard hat, to which was fastened a tallow dip incased in clay, while three more dips dangled from the buttons of his coat, and with a little round, wooden box, as thick as a broomstick, in his pocket, filled with matches, he felt a self-importance and pride such as never before had possessed him.

A short walk brought them to the shaft-house. From

the shaft's mouth, a thin cloud of vapor and smoke was slowly rising, and from time to time dull sounds smote upon their ears,— sounds which seemed to come from the remotest depths of the cavernous abyss; and then a fainter sound of dripping water was heard, as it trickled and dropped from the seams and crevices of the hanging-wall rock to the rough bed-planks below.

Edmunds threw back the cover of the man-hole, and told the Finn to go ahead, and Hayden to follow him. He then stepped in after them and lowered the door again over his head. It fell to its place with a heavy thud, which echoed and re-echoed through the great openings below. Having closed the door, and thus checked the strong draft which swept up the ladderway, Lute drew from his pocket the round wooden match-box, and, having lighted his candle, reached down and lighted the one on Hayden's hat.

At this time, "man-engines" and "man-cars" had not been introduced into the mines of the Lake region, and the only method of getting in and out of them was the primitive one of ladders.

Lute placed himself between Hayden and the Finn; and with a few words of caution to Hayden, in which he told him to keep a firm grasp with his hands on the rungs of the ladder, and not to let go his hold until he felt firm footing for his feet— for if a rung should be broken or missing his foot would find it out first— they commenced to descend. The Finn, accustomed to the descent by long service in the mine, made nothing of his load, and went down at a rapid rate; and Lute, with his long legs, wiry muscles, and little flesh, had no difficulty in keeping close to him. Hayden had been a good athlete at college, but climbing a sloping ladder was a new kind of exercise for him, and it required some exertion on his part to keep up with the others. Yet he would not be outdone by them, at least in so simple a matter as climbing *down* a ladder; so when they stopped for a moment at the sixth level, they found him close behind them.

Down to this point, and, indeed, for a few levels below, the copper-bearing portions of the vein had been "worked out," and the levels and "backs" had been abandoned to the rats and the mould. In many places here the levels were choked and filled with great masses of fallen rock, and timbers that had rotted and fallen away, or had been crushed by the weight that had been put upon them. The air in these places was dead and foul. Men seldom went into them, as indeed they had no occasion to do. In fact, they were forbidden to do so unless ordered, for the danger from falling rock was great; while the danger of setting fire to the accumulations of timber and decayed wood was a constant menace to the mine itself, and to the men who were in it.

Lute had stopped to see how Hayden was enduring the unwonted labor, but upon his assurance that he felt no fatigue and was thoroughly enjoying it, they continued their descent. The ladders, which near the surface were wet and slimy, were now dry, and there was no longer any sound of dripping water in the shaft. The air was drier, and the currents hardly perceptible. The temperature was more even, and they noticed the smell of fresh powder-smoke rising in the ladder-way; they heard, too, the dull reverberations of the blasts away below them, like the booming of distant cannon, sometimes at intervals, and again following one another in quick succession.

Hayden became elated with the novelty of the situation, and, as his spirits rose, he quickened his step and began to whistle a lively air. Suddenly he was startled by a loud hallooing and shouting from the Finn. He stood still on the ladder, and looked down to see what was the matter. Edmunds also had stopped, and was looking at the Finn in amazement. The latter had put down his load and was gazing up at them, gesticulating with both hands and talking in loud and excited tones, but in such a diabolical mixture of bad English and unknown Finnish, that it was utterly impossible to understand what he was trying to communicate. At length, however, a light seemed to dawn upon Edmunds, and his temper, which was easily excited, flared up at the Finn.

"You roaring idiot, what are you doing there, blowing away like a spouting whale? Do you think you are going to fall off the ladder and into the shaft, because a man in the mine happened to whistle a bit, or are you afraid a wad from a missed hole in some of these old backs will blow out and hit you while you are passing? Pick up your load now, and travel on, or I'll drop one of these rocks down on to your thick stupid head."

The poor man, more frightened than ever, hastily took

up his instruments and slid down the ladder, talking to himself the while in a lingo wholly unintelligible to the others. To Hayden's inquiry, "what on earth ailed the fellow?" Lute replied, that a strong superstition prevailed among the miners that it was an unlucky thing to whistle in the mine, consequently they never did it, nor allowed others to, if they could help it. There was no harm in singing, but whistling was sure to bring them bad luck.

The man did not stop until he had reached the bottom of the ladder at the twelfth level. Here he waited for them. They had now reached the depth where active mining operations were in process, and Edmunds led the way into the level over which "stopers" were breaking down the vein. Their lights glimmered dimly in the smoky air, like stars seen through a cloudy sky; and the measured ring of their hammers, as they struck the drills, fell upon the ear in sharp cadence.

"Halloo, there!" shouted Edmunds in a loud voice.

"Halloo!" came the answer from above.

"Let nothing down," cried Edmunds.

"All right."

"Has Captain Wick been here this morning?"

"Yes, was in 'ere with Cap'n Bill, not more 'n a 'alf 'our ago."

"Which way did they go from here?"

"Dunno, couldn't say, but b'leeve a must 'ave gone down er shaft to the fourteenth, as we 'eared Cap'n Bill say 'ee must measure up Dick Trevarrow's drift south er number two."

With this information they started to retrace their steps to the shaft, but found their way partially blocked by a party of timbermen who were pulling a large stull timber into the cutting-out stope beyond them. With tackle and blocks made fast to a brace secured over the level, they were hauling it in sailor fashion over the rough bottom of the drift, to the tune of—

Heave! Heave! Ho! Ho! Heave! Heave! Ho! Ho!

Heave! Heave! Ho! Ho! Heave! Heave! Ho! Ho!

Many of the men had deep, musical voices, and as there were both bass and tenor singers among them, the effect was weird and pleasing.

Waiting until the men had seen them, and had desisted from their work to let them pass, they climbed over the timber and went on their way. Down the shaft for two more "lifts" brought them to the lowest level of the mine. From this level the new openings were being pushed in each direction. The several shafts were "sinking" below it, and from each of them the levels which should connect them all together were being extended north and south.

At this level, a few feet from the shaft, a party of miners were seated upon bits of board or blocks of timber, eating their luncheon. They were Cornishmen, and the Cornish miner is always a good liver. Each man had a tin dinner-pail, which he had placed upon a rude support of bits of broken stone, and under it had lighted the ends of three or four tallow dips, with which he was warming his tea. From a tray which fitted into his pail, he produced a "pasty" (meat pie), liberal slices of bread and butter, several boiled eggs, and a huge piece of saffron cake. With soiled hands and faces begrimed with smoke and dirt, but with appetites sharpened by hard labor, these sturdy miners, down in the dark caverns of the earth, ate like country squires at a feast; then for a brief space they smoked their pipes in quiet contentment. Little was said by them, though occasionally rough jokes were bandied about. Rats would run squealing past them, and often stop at a little distance away to eat the bits of bread and meat which the men would throw to them. The men always petted and fed them; and at times the rats would become quite tame, and eat almost from their hands. They would come so near that certain ones were recognized and named, always with high-sounding titles, such as the "Duke of Wellington," "General Grant," or the "Queen of Sheba." They were never frightened or driven away, for a superstition (much like that among sailors, that rats always leave a sinking ship) formerly prevailed among miners, that when the rats left a mine it was time for the men to get out of it too.

These men recognized Edmunds, as it was his business to make the underground surveys and he was often among them.

They greeted him with a "Good mornin', Master Edmunds, how are ye gettin' on?"

"All right, boys, how are you? Did you see the captains pass this way?"

"Yes, they was 'ere not ten minutes ago, but said they couldn't wait, and told us to tell 'ee when 'ee come, that the drift they wanted the levels on was the thirteenth, north er number four. Will 'ee sit down a bit, Master Edmunds, and touch er pipe er bit?"

"No, thank you, boys, we must get up to the thirteenth, and over to number four, or we will not get out before afternoon. I'm sorry I have missed the captain, as I don't know just what he wants done. He said last night he would meet me at the shaft. What party is working that drift, do you know? Are the day-shift men there now?"

"Yes, I s'pose, for we 'eered Cap'n Wick tell Cap'n Bill that he b'leeved they men had run they drift too high, and he ordered 'em to stop work til you coomed round."

With this information, Edmunds and his little party began the ascent to the next level. He was vexed at missing the captain and having to retrace his steps, with the consequent loss of time and added labor that it entailed.

Hayden soon found that going up was not so easy a matter as coming down, and, for the first time in his life, he was surprised to find that his weight was so great! The Finn was the only one that appeared not to notice the change; he went up at about the same speed with which he had come down, even with the load on his back. Edmunds had had too much experience not to know the folly of haste at such work, so he climbed slowly, and apparently without much effort or fatigue.

Having reached the level above, they proceeded through it to the north, passing the number three shaft, and then the number four. About one hundred feet beyond this shaft a winze was being sunk to the level below, and it was now some fifty feet deep. The rock from it had not been trammed away for three or four days, and lay scattered about in the level, making the walking over it rough and difficult. Immediately around the mouth of the winze it was piled up to the height of two or three feet, requiring a good deal of stooping on the part of the men to avoid striking their heads against the roof of the level. To make it worse, the miners had just hoisted up three or four buckets full of muddy, slimy water, and dumped it over the rock.

Edmunds and Hayden by much caution had picked their way safely over it. The Finn, some distance behind them, was clumsily plodding along under his load and had just reached the top of the pile, when they heard him cry out. Edmunds turned quickly, just in time to see the man's foot slip from under him, and leave him sprawling at full length among the stones. His tripod was flung back against the wall of the drift, and his instrument, striking once against the collar planking, slid off and fell heavily into the winze. The Finn, too frightened and dazed to think of anything better to do, picked himself up, and stood staring stupidly about him.

Edmunds had seen his precious property disappear, and had instantly realized the probable damage and delay it would cause him. He was a passionate man, and never minced words when his temper was roused; but the thing had come so suddenly, had been so quickly done, that for a moment he was unable fittingly to express the rage and disgust that boiled within him. For an instant only he glared with flaming eyes at the stupid fellow, and then, reaching out both hands, he made a mad rush to catch him by the collar. But the Finn, though slow of gait and heavy of wit, had the instinct of an animal for self-defense and protection. He saw at once that lightning was unchained, that a thunderbolt was about to burst forth; but he had no intention that it should fall on him. So, just as he was expected to receive the shock, with all his solid, stolid bulk he threw himself with surprising agility flat on the ground, and rolled quickly to the side wall of the level, and lay there, crowded close against it.

The effect of this sudden disappearance of his victim was different from what the surveyor had anticipated, for, finding no obstacle to arrest the force of his reckless onslaught, he tripped, stumbled, and then fell headlong, face downwards, among the rocks and mud.

Edmunds slowly raised himself to his feet, stunned a little, but swearing like a Turk, and fuming like a maddened bull. His appearance was ridiculous in the extreme. His clothes and face were covered with mud, and blood was dripping from his nose and from a cut in his forehead. His rage before he fell had been furious; now it was cyclonic! As soon as he was able to stand firmly on his feet again, he looked for the Finn, but that individual, with all his dulness, was too shrewd a fellow to be found by him within battling distance, after such a catastrophe. It happened that the hoisting-bucket was down, and the fellow, with the nimbleness of a cat, had sprung to the rope, and lowered himself to the bottom, where he now was, in close companionship with three of his sturdy countrymen.

Failing to discover him, Edmunds at once suspected the manner of his disappearance. He stepped to the platform, and leaning on the windlass, looked down into the pit. There he saw his enemy, safe from harm, though not sheltered from the torrent of invective and abuse which Edmunds proceeded to pour out upon him.

"You d—d, web-footed, fish-eating, blubber-soaked porpoise, what are you doing down there? It's well for you that you went down when you did, for if I had caught you here, I would have flung you down head foremost, as you did my transit. Have you found it, you blockhead? Is it smashed to smithereens, you crocodile? Come, fish around and find it, and bring it up to me. If it's broken, you shall pay for it, or I will take it out of you. You ought to be skinned and your tough hide tanned to make shoepack leather."

To all this the Finn answered never a word, and his companions also preserved a discreet silence. Edmunds, knowing well that they would never come up while he remained there, and having by this explosion appeased his wrath in large measure, told Hayden, that as it would now be impossible for them to proceed with their work, there was nothing left for them to do but to return to the surface. So, retracing their steps, to the shaft, they began the climb. Edmunds, as before, climbed slowly,— a fortunate thing for Hayden, for to one unaccustomed to it this mode of exertion is very laborious. It is only by practice that one learns, in climbing ladders, to avoid unnecessary strains, to sustain one's weight in the easiest manner, and to incur the least amount of fatigue.

As it lacked an hour of noon there was no need for haste, and after climbing for a couple of "lifts," Edmunds would sit for a few minutes to rest, and, as he said, "to catch his wind." During one of these intervals, his ruffled spirits having once more resumed a tranquil state, he alluded apologetically to what had passed, and said that he feared Hayden might form a wrong opinion of him because of their brief acquaintance, and his limited knowledge of his peculiarities. He was not of vindictive disposition, he said, and his temper, which was often quickly aroused, usually spent itself as quickly, and left no trace behind; "and after all," he continued, "the poor devil was not to blame, he couldn't help it. Why, I slipped myself as I was passing the winze, and came near falling in. I suppose the captain will want to discharge him, but I'll see to that, I won't have him discharged. I would rather have him as a helper now than another man. This thing will make him careful, and he will never have an accident of that sort again."

Hayden assured him that he knew that he meant the man no harm; that it must have been exceedingly exasperating; and that he himself would have been very angry, had such an accident happened to him; — and so they resumed their climb.

In fact, however, Hayden had been so intensely amused with the whole performance, which he thought as good as a play, that it had been with the greatest difficulty that he had been able to control himself, and to keep from exploding with laughter. So now, as he slowly followed Edmunds up the ladder, he laughed long and heartily, though necessarily without noise. During the monotonous climb from level to level, talking was more or less difficult, and each was left to his own reflections.

As they were ascending by way of the pump-shaft, they could hear the trickling of the water as it ran down under the ladders, and was led through gutters into the "sumps," or cisterns, made to receive it. By their side was the heavy iron water column which led to the surface, and above it worked the clumsy wooden pump-rods, now moving slowly back and forth, and forcing upwards a dirty stream to the daylight and fresh air above them.

Hayden from time to time questioned his companion as to the methods employed for getting the water out of the mine, and asked the reason for certain appliances which he did not fully understand. To all these questions Edmunds replied as best he could, and often stopped to explain more minutely such points as were complicated or obscure. Hayden was greatly interested in it all, and was determined to understand thoroughly every part of the underground work and manipulation. Thus it was nearly noon, when, coming up into the second level, they found the two captains sitting on a tool-box, leisurely smoking their pipes, while they consulted together about the work of the day.

"Halloo, Lute," said Captain Bill, as soon as the surveyor had emerged from the ladder-way, "we've been hoping to come across ye all the morning. Did yer put the levels in for the drift men in the bottom north of number four?"

At the first mention of the work which he was expected to have done, Edmunds's wrath blazed up again. It was a matter of pride with him to keep faithfully all appointments, and the responsibility for a failure was always something to be put on another's shoulders, if possible. In this case he was so clearly not at fault that the captain's question acted like a spark to a magazine, and the explosion followed quickly.

"No, I have not taken the levels; we went there for it, and just as we were ready to begin work, that miserable, benighted, coffee-colored devil of a Finlander you sent me dumped my instrument into the winze. It's a pity the old leatherhead had not tumbled in after it. What did you send me such a stupid fool for? He couldn't understand anything I said to him, and is no good anyway for any work I have to be done."

"Well, Lute," said Captain Wick, "why did n't ee tell me what ee wanted? I thought yer only wanted a man to pack yer tools for 'ee, and 'ee's good 'nuff for that anyway. Where is 'ee now? Damme, man, I'll discharge un soon as ever 'ee cooms to surface."

"I don't know where he is; the last I saw of him, he was in the bottom of the winze, squatting down behind three other blubber-eating donkeys. I suppose he's there yet.

At any rate you won't see him again to-day."

"Won't I though?" responded the captain, beginning to get excited in his turn. "I'll find um before 'ee goes 'ome tonight, and I'll send un to the hoffice with 'iss time, first thing to-morrow morning'. I tell 'ee I will!"

"Who told you to give the man his time? I didn't tell you to discharge him."

"You told me 'ee's no good, and said I no business send ye such a man. If 'ee's no good for ye, 'ee's no good for we. I tell 'ee, 'ee shall 'ave 'iss time, 'ee shall go to-morrow morning'. Damme, man, think I'll 'ave a man workin' in this 'ere mine that 'll drop engineer's hinstrument down er shaft? Why 'ee might er broke th' 'eads av they men in er bottom, if th' skulls had n't been too 'ard to crack."

"I say, Captain, I won't have him discharged. It was n't his fault."

"It was n't his fault!" shouted the captain. "You said 'ee flung yer hinstrument down er winze; pray tell me 'oose fault was it, if it was n't 'iss? Was it yourn? Damme, man, if I know how to make 'ee out at all!"

"No, it was n't his fault," reiterated Edmunds. "It was the fault of his stupid countrymen, working in the winze. You see the trammers hadn't taken away the rock for two days, and the night men had hoisted their water, and dumped it on the pile; and, in trying to get over it with his load, the fellow slipped and fell, and the instrument was knocked out of his hand, and slid into the winze. It's a wonder he did n't go in himself, for I came very near falling in. It's a shame to leave things in that way. The fellow was not to blame at all; I wouldn't have him discharged. I have no doubt he has a wife and a big family of children in the old country, depending on him for their bread, and it would be a downright cruelty to discharge him for that."

"Well, then, I'll discharge they men in er winze; they no business to dump they water on th' rock-pile."

"No, you won't discharge the men in the winze; it was n't their fault; if you let your trammers leave the rock until it fills up the level, what are they going to do with their water? They can't dump it anywhere else and they can't leave it in the winze! It looks to me, Captain, as if it was more your fault than any one's else!"

"Well, damme, man," shouted the now irate captain, "what the 'ell do 'ee want me to do, — discharge myself?"

At this juncture, Captain Bill, seeing that the discussion had proceeded far enough, and having, by reason of it, reached a pretty clear understanding of the affair himself, namely, that it was purely an accident for which no one could be held accountable, deemed it best to terminate the dispute before anything more serious should come of it. So, rising hastily, he ordered Captain Wick to "climb," and, quickly following him, they all took to the ladders and began ascending at a pace much more rapid than that at which Edmunds had led Hayden thus far.

The latter soon found that the captains were a hard pair to follow, and that his wind was being put to the test as never before. Edmunds with his lean body and sinewy legs, accustomed to the ladders, quickened his steps without difficulty. Faster and faster they went, until their pace became almost a run.

It soon dawned upon Hayden that he was their victim, and that they were trying to tire him out before he could reach the surface. He resolved to outwit them if possible. He had always been good in athletic sports, and he had very soon learned, as they were slowly climbing the levels below, the easiest position to take in ascending. He said nothing, but followed them quietly, keeping close to Edmunds's heels. He soon discovered that the surveyor was puffing and wheezing like a locomotive, that he was putting forth his utmost exertion to keep up with the captains, and that his feet struck the rungs of the ladder with a nervous and uncertain tread. This encouraged him, for he had no difficulty in following; except for his quickened breathing, he gave no evidence of fatigue, and his muscles were supple and firm. He saw, too, that the captains had reached their limit of speed, and he felt no fear that he should fail in the race.

On they pushed, and, as their steps rang out in unison, the ladders creaked and groaned with every fall of their feet. Edmunds's breathing became more labored and hurried with each step, and his feet fairly trembled as they struck the rounds of the ladder. The captains, too, were breathing harder, as Hayden could hear above the sound of the creaking ladder.

With a hasty glance upward he saw a glimmer of daylight through the open man-hole at the shaft-house. It was not more than forty feet above them; but would

Edmunds be able to reach it? Hayden feared for him, but not for himself; for the surveyor had begun to lag, and the space was lengthening between him and Captain Bill, who was next ahead of him. They were rapidly nearing the top, but the space between Edmunds and the captain was increasing fast, and his trembling legs fairly shook the ladders. He seemed about to give out, when Hayden shouted to him to push on, as he was almost up; and he threw all his remaining strength into one last frantic effort to reach the goal.

Captain Wick shot through the man-hole with Captain Bill close after him. Edmunds, with one spasmodic lunge, threw his arms through the opening, and his head and shoulders dropped limp and helpless on the floor of the shaft-house. The two captains seized him by the arms, pulled him up, and set him on a block of wood, where he remained in a state of collapse for ten minutes or more.

Hayden had bounded lightly through the man-hole as soon as Edmunds was pulled out of it. Captain Bill grabbed him by the hand. "You have done well, old fellow," he said. "We were determined to give you a good rattle, and we did it, but by gill, you're a trump! Why, you are a perfect horse! I believe you'd break down the captain and me. We'll never try that on you again. But poor Lute, I don't know but we've killed him! Halloo, there, Lute, how are you gettin' on? Are you dead, old fellow?"

Lute had now recovered himself somewhat, and straightening up, he answered:

"No, I'm all right. It was because I didn't eat any breakfast this morning. I was faint for want of food. I could have followed you up from the bottom at that rate, if it had n't been for that."

The captains looked knowingly at each other and smiled, but made no reply, while Lute slowly rose to his feet, and proceeded to follow them to the changing-house.

Hayden's reputation with the mine captains and for all underground operations was established, once and for all. He was triumphant. He had gained a complete victory, a victory over a prejudice: the prejudice of strength against skill, of brawn against brain.

BACKFURROW

LIFE down on the Michigan farm, even in the 20th century, often proved little more than a struggle for existence. Backbreaking work from dawn to dusk, a constant battle against nature and market conditions and the tedium of an isolated, uncultured environment were only too often the fate of farm men and women alike.

When the 20th century brought increased industrialization to many sections of Michigan, better paying jobs in automobile plants and other factories lured thousands of young people off the farm. But for those who stayed, the benefits of rural living, clean air and plenty of fresh food seemed reward enough for their toil.

Geoffrey Dell Eaton published in 1925 a novel that portrayed the bleak life on a central Michigan farm during the 1920's. BACKFURROW, though little known, has been termed a "milestone in the development of American realism". The New York publishing firm of G.P. Putnam's Sons accepted 31 year old Eaton's first novel for publication while George Haven Putnam was in Europe. When Putnam read the novel he was shocked by Eaton's realistic portrayal of rural manners and morals. After the author made some concessions, the publisher printed the novel but forbade all publicity and did not allow the book to be sold in any of its retail stores. Despite positive reviews, BACKFURROW soon dropped out of sight. Eaton became editor of PLAIN TALK magazine in 1927. He died early in life, never completing another novel. BACKFURROW remains one of the most realistic portrayals of the harsher aspects of Michigan farm life.

Backfurrow

IN a cluster of hills of mid-Michigan lay a fifty acre farm, with the original old worm rail fences marking it off from the neighboring and larger farms, which stood on more level ground, the slopes bordering the small farm being left to wood lots. These gave it an added touch of isolation which was hardly relieved by the double row of trees flanking the narrow and seldom traveled road that marked the western limits of the farm.

But there were few trees on the farm itself, the wood lot being reserved to the steepest, stoniest hill. The fight for existence on a small piece of ground, mostly glacial tillite and full of boulders, stones and freshet gullies, permitted little of the land to be wasted. Even the angles of the rail fence were carefully cleared of all brush, except the wild raspberry and blackberry vines. A plow could not turn into these spaces, so they were put to their only possible source of profit. Wire fences would have given more acreage to the fields, and the rude cultivation of the berry bushes showed acknowledgment of this—but the rails zigzagged their course, save for a few breaks where barbed wire, strung on trees, indicated work of repair.

The house occupied a central position near the road which fronted the place. It was old, and its coat of paint probably as old as the house itself, though it was spotted in places where, more recently, new siding had replaced the old and had been given a single coat of white. It was flanked by a woodshed, wagon-shed-and-granary in combination, smokehouse, outhouse, corncrib, chicken house, pig sty and a barn, all in an equal state of dilapidation. In front of the house stood a rock-lined well where a windlass dropped a bucket sixty feet to an ice-cold spring, which often yielded drowned mice, crickets, fallen tree toads and leaves.

On both sides of the house were rickety porches, "stoops," facing east and west. In the summer the building was surrounded by lilac bushes, rambler roses, "lemon" lilies and marigolds, which gave it a picturesque appearance, for all its own ugliness. In winter it was barren and the snow over the manure, heaped around to keep it warm within, sloped up the sides, making it

146

appear more squat and desolate.

But summer and winter the windows remained cracked and broken, the loose shingles of the roof admitted water, and that which ran from the eaves seeped from the cistern into the cellar, which was redolent with the odor of rotting cabbages, turnips, and potatoes, with cider and vinegar barrels, and with spoiled cans of fruit.

A phoebe built its nest every year on one of the beams, using a broken cellar window as means of exit and entrance. Only that part of the house which constituted the "parlor" and living room was cellared. Besides these rooms there were, "downstairs," a bedroom and a pantry; above, two bedrooms and a store-room.

The parlor, facing north, was seldom used. It contained a bed for infrequent guests, and a round stove, which was employed when the weather became excessively cold, in addition to the stove in the living room. There was also in the parlor a bookcase, a deer's head badly stuffed, a shelf of bric-a-brac and two horse-hair chairs. In the bookcase stood such volumes as Horace Greeley's history of the Civil war, *The Life of General Grant,* agricultural reports from Washington, *The Arabian Nights, The Civil War In Song and Story,* a huge Bible filled with newspaper clippings of births and deaths, cooking recipes, pressed flowers, and dusty locks of hair tied with faded silk ribbons. A small Old Testament and a small New Testament, a Sears-Roebuck catalogue, and a pile of sportsmen's magazines, most of them several years old, completed the collection.

In the living room was a cracked range which served both to heat the house and for the preparation of meals. It was a huge old cast-iron affair with many lids, big oven, and a warming shelf overhead. Its hearth was fully two feet from the floor, and the whole thing was mounted on firm iron legs. Between the back entrance and a door, which opened to an inside flight of steps into the cellar, there was a table, spread with a white cloth of quaint red design, before which, at meal times, were placed several old fashioned wood-bottom chairs. Over a couch, stuffed with straw, there was a shelf holding a silver cup—"second prize" in a rifle meet of fifty years before, a tobacco jar, and a very old clock which struck extremely rapid notes. Screwed into another wall were the headplate and antlers of a deer, and resting thereon was a hammer, "sidelock" shot-gun which had seen many years of service.

The carpet on the floor, like all of the others in the house, was of woven rags, and it was spotted and always smelling of tobacco juice. The wood-box behind the stove smelled also of tobacco, and of tree bark. The odor of the whole room: of burning wood, tobacco, wood bark, cooking food and human bodies, so characteristic of many farmhouses of that time, was not unpleasant; a musty tang that always meant "home" to the country folk, the neighbor, the rural mailman, and the teacher of the district school.

The wall was papered but it hung loose in many places; the pattern is common enough even now, that of tiny scrolls and still tinier specks, conceived by some enterprising person to the end of making fly specks only a part of the design.

There were no pictures on the wall except for two lithographed calendars, and a wee picture framed with and surmounting a mirror.

The bedrooms were all much the same, housing black walnut beds with straw "ticks" and patchwork quilts.

The store-room above was filled with many things, and was a favorite haunt for the cat when it was bent on catching mice—which confined themselves to this room and to the cellar, whence they made their nocturnal forays. In this room strings of herbs hung to the walls, with seed corn and old clothes. Despite the broken window and the door, partly opened, to accommodate the cat, there was a strong smell of all the dusty things, the most noticeable of which was that from catnip— which probably led to many gratuitous mousing expeditions. In the room were also bags of nuts and popcorn, bundles of old clothes and rags for making carpets, several piles of old newspapers, and a reloading set for shotgun cartridges. A palace for a pair of busy young hands and eyes on rainy days.

On a July morning a boy stood on the rear porch of the farmhouse, looking through the scant apple orchard at the figure of his grandfather "cultivating" the potatoes in the field beyond. He heard his commands to the horse, his profanity when the little blades of the cultivator caught on rocks and threw man and implement to one side.

As he looked and listened the boy drifted in dreamy thought, a thing which he did constantly, a thing which caused some of the neighbors to call him half-witted. But one could see from the finely shaped head, the straight nose, the intelligent deep blue eyes, the sensitive mouth and intellectual little chin that he was no half-wit. In spite of his meagre twelve years he had a decided personality.

His characteristics were no heritage from his grandfather. They had come obviously from his father's side. His father was unknown, for the boy had not been born of wedlock and at the time of his birth there had been a scandal on the countryside though such an occurrence was nevertheless frequent enough in that region. The old man's daughter, his only daughter, had left the baby and her home.

The grandfather had given the boy his own name, Ralph Dutton, but not until after a period of conflict and doubt, and not until the solemn smile of the baby had won him completely over.

Under the care of the old man and his wife the boy grew, went to school, and helped about the farm and house. He became devoted to both old Dutton and his wife, and he was early instructed to call them "Grandpa" and "Granny." The old man became a hero in the boy's eyes, and the lad tried to imitate him in everything. He cried once because his grandfather would not allow him to run the cultivator.

"It would yank your guts out," said the old man in refusing. And he was right. Operating a one-horse cultivator without wheels on a stony and hilly farm calls for the inertia of a heavy body and the resiliency of an extremely muscular one.

But the boy sowed timothy, clover, wheat, planted corn and potatoes, "mowed away" the hay and grain in the barn, cut corn, milked the cows, churned, brought in wood. When he was not busy at some of these tasks he often took his bow and arrow into the woods where he would lie and think for hours at a stretch.

In spite of all of his dreaminess he had a resentful

temper, which, however, had a habit of remaining unexpressed, calming suddenly at its highest point. Sometimes it burst through, but this was not often. Otherwise he would have been in continual trouble at school. As he was poorly dressed and went barefoot from April until November he was often the butt of jokes. It was, perhaps, the innate cruelty of children, of his schoolmates which gave the unconscious philosophical turn to his temper. The other children were constructed differently; when they were jibed at they were sheepish but good-natured. Ralph was resentful but silent.

At first he was dressed better, for his mother sent money, from Detroit, then from Toledo, and later from Buffalo, but one day his grandfather received a letter which advised him that his daughter was "street-walking," and after that the old man sent back the next remittance and wrote his daughter fiercely to "keep your dam dirty money."

Then, later, came a message that his daughter was very sick, and while he was struggling with his Biblical training and refraining from writing to her, she died. The body was shipped home and interred in the local cemetery. This was according to the daughter's last request and was provided for by what little money she had—for the old man would have nothing to do with the matter, and refused to let her body be buried in the family plot. The event revived the scandal and placed Ralph more open to the thoughtless remarks of his schoolmates. This, however, had occurred when he was ten years of age, and the disagreeable aftermath had not been long.

Every year or two there was an illegitimate child born in the township and the subject was tender and likely to hit someone else at the school. Thus he suffered less than he might have. There was "Big" Gamble, the "bully" of the school who had a three year old niece whose father was unknown, and "Big" was very prompt to cuff a head or two if such a subject were brought up.

The boy thought vaguely on this thing at times. He thought of it now as he kicked his feet in the dust around the porch. It was an uncomfortable feeling. It was forever linked with the things the boys wrote on the side of the schoolhouse, things that they laughed over half ashamed, half boastful, things the teacher caned them for when they were caught. It must be all bad, the boy concluded, and he set off to trudge along behind his grandfather.

He came up behind the old man and though the latter was aware of his presence he neither turned nor spoke until the end of the row was reached. His task required every bit of his attention, but when he came to the fence he stopped the horse.

"Hello, Ralphie," he said. "What have you been doin this mornin'?"

"Nothin'."

"This work tuckers me all out," said the old man. He took his hat off and wiped his forehead with his sleeve. Under his arms great damp circles showed in the blue cloth of his shirt.

"The sun's gittin' hot. I can't stand this work many years longer. After I start this row, run down to the corner and under that scrub oak you'll find the water bottle. Fetch it back so I can have a swig when I come back. I wish we'd git rain." He adjusted the cultivator and spoke to the horse, and man and beast went plodding down the field.

There had been no rain in weeks and the potatoes had been affected. The drought was already beginning to brown and curl the leaves of the plants. In the spring there had been so much rain that the seed had soured and rotted in the ground, and only about two-thirds of them had sprouted. Others had been put in their places and they were just now showing above the surface; they would be late and small.

When the boy returned with the demijohn containing the water bottle the old man had reached the other end of the field and was turning to come back. The boy became speculative. How many times, he asked himself, did his grandfather or himself walk up and down a row of potatoes each year? He began to count up. Three times when plowing. Of course, dragging and marking covered three rows at a time, but the field had to be cross-dragged and cross-marked, and so nearly once to each row. And then in planting seeds he and his grandfather walked the length of the field to plant two rows each. Then they had to be cultivated six or eight times a season, a row at a time; and gone over some by hand where the implement failed to catch the weeds, two rows at a time; and then they had to be sprayed with Paris green five or six times, again two rows at a time. Generally they picked the bugs once or twice a year in addition. In the fall they had to dig the potatoes, two rows at a time. And then they had to pick them. That was the job! The boy thought of how they went bending over, half of the time plowing along on their knees. Never did anything so tire him.

Twenty times or more to each season each row had to be gone up and down. And then came blights and droughts, and like as not the crop was only about half what it ought to be. And then, the year they had such a good crop, such fine potatoes, they couldn't get ten cents a bushel and the potatoes had to be fed to the hogs.

What a terrible lot of work! And how hard the work was! No walking was so rough. City visitors coming to fish for trout mopped their faces after walking across a plowed field. Well, the walking *was* rough. The boy decided that wading through two feet of snow was easier than walking across a plowed field, and he walked a mile to school many times during the winter in one, two, and sometimes nearly three feet of snow.

In running the plow, cultivator, and drag, how his grandfather had to brace his body all of the time, toeing out with his feet! Ralph had noticed that the city men never walked like the farmers. The upper half of the farmer's body curved both forward and back, his hands, unused to idleness, flopped grotesquely around, his haunches were always braced, his legs slanted forward; and he always toed out. The city man's foot was directed straight.

His grandfather came up swearing; the horse had stepped on several plants and the cultivator in glancing from the rocks had uprooted several more. The old man had had to stop and replace these.

"Damn farmin'!" he said. "No man works so hard with so little pay. And blights and droughts, plants burnin' up and seed sourin' in the ground. Sometimes I think there ain't no God."

Ralph winced a little at these words. The old man was generally devout and the boy was brought up on the

Bible. "Elmer Fox makes money," said he timidly.

"Yes, he makes money. And what from? From his hired men, that's what. Hires 'em in the summer, eight dollars a month, cheaper if he can git 'em, and fires 'em in the winter. He's got two hundred acres, flat ground, gang cultivators, disc harrows, three horses, mowers, binders, drills, and everything else. Him and his men each farms three rows where I farm one."

He threw the cultivator around sharply and started down the row again, swearing. Ralph wondered a bit at the incongruity of prayers at every meal and this extreme profanity. Sometimes the old man got "full." He watched his grandfather's body sag, sway, and brace. He saw the scant gray hair under the black felt hat. Without knowing why, Ralph felt tears come into his eyes.

The old man was a mixture of things human. He loved the boy to the verge of foolishness, yet he rarely bought him anything; he was kind to the animals, yet he tied the horse to a tree and beat the animal with an ox-chain because it had run away. He was seldom considerate of his wife, and any word of complaint, any attempt at argument on her part was ruthlessly cut short with a harsh word or so. This, despite the fact that she rarely said anything at all.

In the town his stocky five feet ten was greatly feared by some of the men, yet his kind eyes, his straggly mustache, his blunt chin, his broken nose and shaggy white eyebrows, was a picture for the town boys to venerate. They loved him. To all of them he was "Uncle Ralph." His temper seemed to flare only at mature beings.

Most of the time he got along well enough with the men, but sometimes, after drinking a little, he fought with them. In one night he had dealt out awesome punishment to the three "best" men in the town, one after the other. All over some trivial altercation.

After such fights he would drink until he could hardly stagger to his horse and "rig." Then he would fumblingly tie the reins to the whip-socket. "Go home, Nig," he would say to the horse, and home they inevitably went, no matter how dark the night, the old man singing the songs of his youth at the top of his voice.

The boy and his grandmother, on such occasions, would hear him when he was more than a half mile from the house, his half-shrill, half-croaking voice coming ghost-like out of the night. They invariably sat up for him and invariably went to meet him, with a lantern. He was nearly always good-natured at such times. Never did his wife say a word against such proceedings. Either then or in the morning. At the breakfast table, following these periodic sprees the old man was exceedingly lengthy in prayers and graces. Not knowing how to add to any one prayer, he would say two or three, or perhaps they would kneel while he read from the Bible.

The boy dimly visualized some of these scenes as he watched. He wished that his grandfather would be a better man.

Again the old man came up the row and stopped at the end. He pulled out the old silver watch tied by a leather thong to a buttonhole in his shirt.

"Eleven o'clock," he said. "I can't stand this any longer. I'm all tuckered out." His knees wavered as he unhitched the horse. After turning the animal loose in the pasture the two went into the house.

"A dram of whiskey will about fix me," said the old man. He went to the cupboard. In a moment or two his vigor returned, but he sat smoking until his wife announced dinner.

The three sat at the little table, which was pressed against the wall. Vegetables were steaming: new potatoes, "string" beans, peas. There were salt meat, homemade bread, golden butter, and honey. There were several kinds of desserts: pie, cake, cookies.

Everything was nicely cooked. The meal was, in fact, excellent. It was at meals that the old man became most expansive. Only at such times, or during an occasional hunting or fishing trip did he praise country life.

"Nothing like living on a farm. Have our own vegetables and eggs and butter. Ever'thing fresh. None of your city junk. No peaked faces on this place. No one to tell you when to start working or when to stop."

Yet the old man never rose later than six, summer or winter; generally about five in the summer and during haying time he was up at four. He frequently cut hay with his scythe until nine at night, when darkness compelled him to quit. The farm was too hilly and stony for a mowing machine or binder; the hay and grain were cut by hand, with scythe or cradle, and all of the corn was cut, stalk for stalk, by hand also.

Ralph often thought about the work connected with the hay. A whole field was reserved for hay, and another for pasture, just to feed the horse, that the horse might draw the plow, drag and wagon. What a lot of work to feed the horse! Then there had to be oats for the horse; another whole field, though they sold half of this crop. Then corn for the horse and the hogs, cornstalks and pumpkins for the cattle. It seemed that they spent half of the time and land supporting the animals.

Ralph was thinking of something of the kind now, when his grandfather interrupted his thoughts.

"Here, Ralphie, dig into this salt pork. It'll grow hair on your belly. And you'll weed the corn the better for it this afternoon."

The old man, though he relished his meals and became more cheerful over them, rarely praised his wife. "Ruth is a good old woman," he might say once in a while, but no more than that. When he thought about her he must have appreciated what she did; he was simply accustomed to having her around, doing things. He saved and planned not half so carefully as she. It was her savings from the eggs and butter that represented the little reserve supply for the frequent purchases of clothing, for doctor bills and emergencies, for buying certain necessities during the winter. It was she who picked berries with Ralph and sold them in the town, and it was she who gave the boy an occasional five or ten cent piece to spend or to hide away in a secret place underneath the corncrib. The three lived in a highly symbiotic relationship the whole season through, but the hardest lot was the woman's.

The short, pathetic romance of the days following the Civil War, when Ralph Dutton, garbed in a blue uniform, came back to woo her, was but a dim memory. When Memorial Day came and the old man dressed for parade in town she would sometimes sigh.

If the endless drudgery of the household occasionally appalled her she gave little evidence of it. Her slight body was in a continual rush about the house. Considering the fact that the men brought in dirt and were slovenly with their spitting, throwing their clothes about, and leaving newspapers scattered around, and that an itinerant son came home and sprawled lazily about the place several months each winter, cluttering up things worse than ever, she kept the house fairly neat and clean.

She spoke little, complained little, and Ralph was greatly astonished to hear her exclaim one day, while his grandfather was in the fields, "Oh, Lordy, Goddy, if I could only get away from this for a while!" These words summed up her grievances in a pitiful, weak, hopeless voice.

As long as Ralph could remember she had never been away from the place over night. There were always the stock, the garden, the poultry, the window plants, the milk, the butter, to be looked after. Sometimes his grandfather went to Detroit, or Grand Rapids, or Kalamazoo, or Battle Creek for several days, but she never got away. Once, indeed, the old man had gone to Washington to a G.A.R. reunion.

She had a number of quaint, homely, oftentimes vulgar, but really not offensive expressions. "Hedgeons!" she would sometimes exclaim. Announcing meals she would say, "Hurrah for dinner!" or, if she was a little tired, simply, "Hurrah!"

At the table Ralph and his grandfather did nearly all the talking, which was not much, and his grandfather did most of that. Sometimes the old man would start on politics and damn Grover Cleveland up and down as a "sneaking rebel," though Cleveland had long been out of office. The worst combination of epithets he could hurl at a man in the public eye was that the office holder was a "Democrat, a Catholic, and an Irishman." The old man himself was of Scotch descent, his wife English, both of a very early pioneering stock.

This day he was visiting his spleen on town veterans who were drawing a larger pension than he, claiming that they had never seen the front, and that some of them were even "bounty jumpers." Some of his complaints on the score were not far from wrong.

"Think of old Al Thurston drawin' thirty-five dollar, and me drawin' only ten. Why, he jumped bounty and went to Canady, and his damned regiment never got below the Kentucky boundary. It wasn't nothin' but a brass band anyhow, and half of 'em deserted when Morgan's men come over the Ohio river on a raid."

He pushed his chair back conclusively, filled his pipe, and went out to the porch. Ralph followed him, and together they went to the cornfield.

"Maybe I'll go back to cultivatin' about three o'clock," said the old man. "I got about two hours' work there yet, and I'd like to git it done afore sun-down, but it's too damn hot now for such work."

In slacker times he was accustomed to rest or take a nap after dinner, but not during the growing season when crops needed the utmost of care. If he was tired he simply did something easier.

They reached the lower end of the cornfield and each fell to weeding a row, pulling those weeds immediately about the hills which the cultivator could not get without also uprooting the corn. Ralph often wondered why it was that weeds were so much hardier than the corn. Why couldn't the corn, he asked himself, choke the weeds out? Or why couldn't the corn grow as naturally as weeds and save people all the work of farming?

He didn't know that corn and potatoes, or any other grain or vegetable, were simply weeds nurtured and evolutionized to a point of greater productivity and tastefulness, although he had often noticed irrelevantly that wild apple trees grew much smaller fruit than those in the orchard.

Nor did he know that the choking-out process was actually used by many farmers who drilled their corn instead of planting it in rows, just as they drilled their wheat and oats. Weeds grow feebly under such conditions, but he had never noticed that. He knew that several farmers drilled corn but he knew also that his grandfather scoffed at that way of growing corn and so, Ralph scoffed at it likewise.

Down the row they went on their knees, plowing along in the dirt. At first they had a race in which Ralph beat his grandfather, getting a whole row ahead of him, but the boy slowly tired and though he spurted now and then, the old man gradually caught up and finally left him far behind. Ralph could not help stopping occasionally to admire the flowers on the wild morning glory vines, which, from the hills, so quickly spread their tendrils across the rows. Three days after cultivating they would be across, and always they climbed and twisted about the growing cornstalks. They were a nuisance, but they were pretty.

There was another weed which he liked in spite of himself. It was a tender plant whose leaves were always jewelled by little globules of moisture and sparkling like tiny diamonds; like the wild morning glory he sometimes disliked to pull it out of the earth. Ragweed he hated, and he hated even more the little, white-flowered milkweed plant whose roots ran straight into the ground for a foot or two, and at which he furiously tussled and tugged, only to have the root break off. He was sure that this plant could never be defeated, that the root would grow another plant in a day or two.

He began to be very hot and sweaty, and finally he attempted to stand up to let the breeze go over him. It was such a delight to stand in the little, vagrant breezes when one was hot and sweaty. It was almost worth working to feel that refreshing coolness. It was especially nice under the arm-pits. But when he tried to stand he couldn't; pains shot through his legs and back, and he started over again, coming very slowly to a standing posture.

"What's the matter Ralphie; got a crimp in you?" called his grandfather. "A spry little feller like you ought to stand it better'n n'old feller like me."

"A long stick bends easier'n a short stick," said Ralph, trying to grin. It was the stock answer to the stock accusation.

He rested until his grandfather could start a new row with him. But when the old man came up, he looked at his watch and decided to cultivate the rest of the afternoon, and he told Ralph to run along and play with his bow and arrow.

Ralph forgot his tiredness and raced up the hills to the house. He got his bow and arrow and his "toad-stabber" knife, and then ran down the lane to the woods. Through them he went, stopping now and then to watch birds, or to sit under a tree sometimes to watch a fox squirrel in the branches high above. He chased a red squirrel down a rail fence, but each diversion he followed by going farther on. There was a pond, a mile forward, near the railroad, where he might find some frogs to shoot, he told himself.

But the real reason for going there was to lie under a tree and watch the trains go by; usually two passenger trains and a couple of freight trains went, in opposite directions, by his vantage point every afternoon between the hours of three and four.

He wondered about the people in the passenger trains, where so many persons were going and coming from, when so rarely he heard of people going on them from his district. But it was the freight trains which especially fascinated him. They seemed so ponderous, so powerful. They stirred unknown emotions within him. There was one engineer on one of them who always waved to Ralph when their afternoons chanced to be the same, and Ralph waved eagerly back, the unknown emotion tugging stronger within him. He would rather be that engineer than be even his grandfather!

That engineer did not go by this afternoon, and Ralph sat quietly for nearly two hours, thinking wistfully of far-off things which he had heard about and could only imagine, making out pictures from the twisting thin clouds, high in the blue sky, or depicting to himself an Indian encampment between a roll in the hills and imagining the braves strutting about, decked profusely with feathers.

Suddenly he realized it was late and he returned reluctantly to take the cows to the stable. He often thought how pleasurable it would be if no one had to work and every one could sit under the trees and dream and think.

TEMPER

HENRY FORD, William Durant, Walter Chrysler and other automotive giants revolutionized the Michigan economy. During the twentieth century the state evolved from a predominatly agricultural bastion into automobile maker to the world. For many the changes wrought by industrialization brought a better life style. Others were caught up in the web of monotonous, demanding factory life that destroyed individuality and character.

Lawrence H. Conrad describes such an experience in TEMPER. Paul Rinelli, an Italian immigrant, begins work in an automobile plant as an ambitious dreamer. His experiences with fellow workers and bosses, the dehumanizing nature of the labor, and the factory itself, the personification of an omnipotent entity, tempers his philosophy about life's values.

Lawrence Conrad was born and raised in Royal Oak. After graduation from high school in 1917 he attended the University of Michigan. In his second year, he ran out of funds and dropped out to work for the Ford Motor Company. As he labored in different departments, operating drill presses and screw machines, "his eyes were open and his mind at work." He also had the opportunity to work with personnel files that held the life stories of thousands of workmen and their families. Conrad recorded these experiences in his first short stories which he sold to help pay for college.

During his senior year at Ann Arbor, Conrad wrote TEMPER. Much of his writing took place in a large busy reading room at the Michigan Union. TEMPER was

160

published in 1924. It won good reviews and went through three editions within two years. The book reviewer of the NEW YORK HERALD — TRIBUNE wrote "here is a primitive among novels; a naive and powerful and simple work...No other writer has so closely approached the modern elementals of a machine age."

Temper

Indignation

IN the morning, Paul got up early, put on his working-clothes and went back to work in the factory. He had been away for a week, and so was a little ashamed when he went to the tool-crib and took out his overalls. But he put them on and then went over and sat on the cover of a waste-can at Bay Twenty-eight. He looked dreamily across into the heart of the department.

The night shift was still at work over there, and most of the machines were running. Along the floor there was no movement, and above only some little part of each one was turning somewhere. His eyes were confused with the forest of belting along the ceiling, and he could see the air thrill with the energy that purred through the streaming leather. Watching the belts for a moment, they would all seem to be pouring downward, down, down in an endless stream. It made him think of words like "forever." Then suddenly, if he just blinked his eyes, the belts would catch him up and whirl him upward so that he would have to gasp at the thought of striking his head on the ceiling.

Down, below, the men moved about slowly. They were clad in one-piece overall suits that covered all of their ordinary clothing. As they bent over their machines, with their black hands sticking out in front of them, they looked like fat bears who had been trained to do tricks by cuffing at levers with their paws.

Here one stood at a bench and pounded upon something with a heavy hammer. You could see every breath he breathed, by the motion of his chest. You could even tell, by the twist of his face, what word it was he said each time the hammer fell. But you could hear no sound of the blow, for it was all taken up with the other noises.

Paul listened to the noises in the same way that he had watched the belting. You could pick up the steady, clean hiss of the lathes, and attach all the other sounds to that. You could make the lathes become the greater part of the shop, and they would stand out from everything else so clearly that while you listened your nostrils would pick up the smell of hot pistons and of an occasional burned tool. But even in that instant, the whole thing would change and you would be able to hear nothing but the rattle of drills, and to smell nothing but the warmish, sickening flavor of the dirty-white cutting-compound, and to taste the grit of soda against your teeth.

Paul looked drowsily at the slow scene before him, and wondered which job they would put him on. It might be the upright lathes again. He watched the big negroes at work there, putting on and taking off the hot pistons with their bare hands. He remembered how he used to glory in being able to handle the hot steel without wincing. But now his fingers crawled up into the palms of his hands and stayed there. The whole process of learning to endure that pain would have to be gone through again. Then he looked across at the lucky fellows who only have to pick up the drilled pistons from the chute, and his hands opened again gladly as they experienced the feel of the cool soda in which the metal is bathed.

There was another thing that he could feel: that beating that always comes inside of you when you are in the factory. It made your heart-beat change, and your breathing change until you got into step with it. Every man's body on every machine swung backward and forward with it—not with each other; with *it,* the beating. It was the thing that the bosses had to change when they wanted to get more production, and they found it a very hard thing to do. It came into you through the floor upon which you stood, through every lever that you put your hand upon, through every breath that you breathed, and even through all of the clamor that kept your ears filled with the good sound of men at work. It came into you through your eyes every minute of the day as you watched every other thing beating in time with it. Some of it came from the touch of the hard, rough foundry-steel that brought it in from another shop, from a mill, from a mine. Perhaps it even lodged there in the machines, which were themselves made somewhere in time to its beat.

When Paul felt it coming over him again, he could tell

what it was doing to him. It was slowing him down; all of his movements, even the movement of his mind. His fine imaginings could not endure in it; they had to move as swiftly as a flashlight. Already as he sat there upon the garbage-can, he could feel the muscles of his legs trembling in response to the vibration that was all about him. He gave attention to his breathing to see if it was still normal. The feeling of the shop was creeping over him like a great dread.

He looked down at his hands and found them half closed, curled around one another, and a feeling in the palms as of levers soon to be grasped. The smell of sweat and tobacco from the men who leaned against the wall near him was pleasant. It brought up old memories of the long, drowsy hours he had spent with his hands doing some senseless thing they had now forgotten, and his mind stagnant and asleep.

When the bell rang, he got down from his seat and went over and stood in front of the foreman.

"Huh!" the old man said. "Well,.what do *you* want?"

"I am ready to come back to work."

"Oh, you are, eh? Ain't that a shame! Do you think we can close the factory every time you get a headache? You go and get your money and clear out."

Paul knew what he would have to say to that. He was ready to take the first step in his long climb.

"I am ready to work awful hard," he said. "Can't you give me some little job like sweeping the floor some place?...I will come to work every day and do what you tell me."

The boss sneered at him. "That is the way to talk," he said. "Now you are beginning to wake up a little bit. Go over and tell Miner to give you a job."

When Miner saw Paul coming, he shook his head. "I can't give you nothin'," he said. "I am all filled up. I will show that old scarecrow that he can't give me any orders. What does he think I am, just some little straw-boss or something?"

The old man came down to where they were talking. "Here is your man back," he said.

Miner shook his head again. "He ain't no good. He makes bad stock and always fights with the men. You shouldn't take him back at all. You ought to fire that kind

163

of a man." The two of them went away under the conveyor together and stood over there arguing and swinging their arms.

When the old man came back, his eyes were bulging and watering, and his thin, freckled hands were shaking. He kept stumbling as he walked along. Paul walked up to the desk with him, and the old man stood blinking at him.

"Let's see," he said. "What were we talking about? Oh, yes; so you want me to give you a job, do you? He tried to wipe the sweat from his forehead, and only made a black streak across it from some grease he had got on his hand. "Well, I will give you a job," he said. "I will show him that I am still the boss here." He looked back towards the conveyor, and there was Miner still looking at him. The old man doubled up his fist and began hitting it on the desk.

"No," he said, "you had better go to work in some other department. I will fix it so you can get a job some place else." He signed his name on a transfer slip and told his clerk to fill it out. Then he looked up and saw Miner laughing at him, so he walked away in the other direction. Paul went after him and took hold of his arm.

"I want to tell you to look out for yourself," he told the foreman. "Some day you are going to forget and raise up when you go under the conveyor. Then you will get killed."

The old man's eyes opened wide, and he began to shake inside of his coat when Paul told him that.

"How do you know that?" he asked eagerly. "Who told you? Who told you that?" He had his hands on Paul's shoulders before he knew it. Then he dropped them quickly and braced himself up.

"You go and get your slip and get to hell out of here. Don't tell me what I ought to do. I can look after my own affairs without any help from you." He threw up his head and went walking down the aisle rapidly, bending his knees like a horse as he walked.

Paul went away with his slip and they transferred him to the steering-gear department. It was on the third floor, and it seemed a great deal lighter up there. The machines were smaller and didn't make so much noise. He stood beside the desk for a while, waiting for a boss to come along. He wondered if they would make him sweep the floor or anything like that.

The boss was an Irish fellow with two gold teeth in the front. He came up and took Paul's card and walked away without saying anything. When he was half way down the aisle he looked back, and then he got mad because Paul wasn't right there following him.

"What's the matter with you, you damn dummy; can't you hear anything, or are you deef?"

"I guess I must have been thinking about something else," Paul told him.

He hurried along beside his new boss until they came to a large gas furnace. Beside it there were two tanks, one of them up high and the other one down on the floor.

"Here," the boss said in Paul's ear, "you work here on this low tank. There is nothing in it but water. All you have to do is to wash the tubes and mind your own business. But you better not let me catch you talking to that Dago on the high tank. He is crazy. He was in jail ten years for killing a policeman. If he comes near you, you had better get away from him."

Paul looked up there and saw a man who was all covered with rubber. He had on a rubber apron and boots and rubber gloves and his face was nearly covered with the shield of his big goggles.

Paul washed tubes all of the morning, and then at noon he waited until the boss had gone out to lunch before speaking to the old man. The fellow was Italian. He was afraid when he saw Paul coming.

"I want you to tell me about that policeman you killed, Paul said to him.

"No, no I never did it," the old man said. "I never killed anybody. There is something the matter, to make everybody afraid of me. But it is wrong. Maybe it is because I got such a good job, and everybody wants it."

"Ho!" Paul said, "that is a good bluff, but you can't fool me. You'd better behave yourself when I am around here. If you ever make a move to touch anybody when I am around, I will drop you right on the spot. You will be a dead one."

The old man's face was working, and he seemed very sad. He had his goggles off, and Paul noticed that he didn't have any eyebrows. His face was yellow. Paul asked him what made it like that.

Ford Motor Co., Detroit, Mich.

Somebody said, "Here comes the boss!" so Paul went and sat down until the bell rang. Then he went to work again.

He kept thinking about the old man, and watching him. He had known some men who talked just like that, and they weren't crazy. They were rather nice old men. If anybody killed a policeman and was sent to jail for it, he would know it. That is a thing you don't forget very easy.

So Paul went on working that way day after day. He had let the men in that department know who he was. They knew their places when they saw him coming. The old crazy man would never come near him after that. He looked as though he were ready to run when Paul looked over at him. The foreman could see that the old dipper was afraid of the young one, and so one day he came and patted Paul on the shoulder.

"You are the kind of a man we need around here," he said. "I am going to get you a raise of forty cents a day."

When Paul went home at night, he would sit and try to read his book. He was such a slow reader that he did not get very far with it. There were so many pages. Often he would catch himself sitting still for a long time, looking up over the book and picturing things when he should have been reading. He would be thinking about things in the shop. What made the old dipper not have any eyebrows? Why didn't he ever go crazy like that, and start some fun?

He would check himself, draw up the book and read some more, and then, in a little while, he would go off thinking again. Why was he such a fool, anyway?—to have a wonderful book right in his hands and not to read it? To have such a fine opportunity for success, and not to take it? What was the matter with Paul Rinelli, anyway? Why didn't he be smart, and read books, and learn how to organize human machinery? Why did he make such good promises to himself every night, and then go back to the shop and act so different in the morning? He could not understand it.

One night he sat thinking about the old crazy man, and wondering how the fellow got to be the kind of man he was. Paul thought that it might be the man's work that had made him that way. He could see a picture in his mind of the old man working there beside the gas furnace, and it was all very interesting. He figured out how the blazing furnace worked: how the endless chain kept running around one side of the furnace and down through the center of it. Then he saw how the men stuck the tubes upright in the chain, and put a heavy flange upon the top of each one. Then the next man put a little handful of brass filings right on top where the tube and the flange came together. The next one put on a pinch of borax for a flux. And all the while the chain was moving along, carrying the tube nearer and nearer to the fire. He watched it go through the flames and saw the brass and the borax melt together and run down a little bit, cementing the flange to the tube. He could hear the roar of the gas furnace, and it seemed as though he were right there in the factory with the old man by his side.

When he awoke in the morning, there was an idea in his head about the old crazy man. He wondered why the old man had to wear rubber clothes in order to dip tubes, when he didn't have to wear any on the same kind of a job. He had a kind of a picture in his mind of the old man taking some tubes from the furnace after they were brazed, and dipping them in the tank. There was always some steam coming up from the high tank. When the old fellow reached down and dropped the tubes into the lower tank, there wasn't any steam. When Paul reached in to take the tubes out of the water, they would be cold. There was something funny about it.

When he got to the factory, he found the old dipper, and went up in the corner where he was.

"I want to know what is in that high tank," he said. "I am not going to hurt you. Just tell me what it is."

The old man shook his head.

"It burns you if you touch it," he said.

Before the bell rang, Paul went over and put his finger in it, and it burned him. When he took it out, it burned worse than when it was in, and before he got it washed off in his own tank, his finger was raw. He thought all day about that wonderful stuff, and at night he went to the little drug store and asked Smith what it could be.

"That is sulphuric acid," Smith said. "If they make you work over a tank full of it, you had better quit."

"What will it do to you?"

"Why, that is a cheap grade of stuff that they use. It has got nitrates in it. That is what makes it give off fumes. And the fumes will burn you. They will hurt your lungs."

"Will they make your skin get all yellow?"

"Yes."

"And will they make your eyebrows come out?"

"I guess they would, after a long time. You better quit that job and go some place else."

"Oh, it is not me. I don't have to work in it, you know. I am a boss over some men. I get around here and there and all over, you see. Oh, don't worry; I wouldn't work on any kind of a job like that."

Sometimes he wondered if Smith believed him. Smith was always ready to think that he had some dirty job in the factory. He wouldn't ask Smith any more questions about the shop.

"I like that book you gave me. I am half through it already."

Smith laughed. "Why, you will be dead before you get an education. You should read a book like that in one day. Why don't you hurry up with it?"

"Yes, I know. I am going home and finish it tonight. Then to-morrow I will come in and report about it."

But when Paul got home and sat down with his book, he began making pictures to himself about Murphy, the Irish foreman with the gold teeth in front.

"That old dipper has got a good job," Murphy had said. "Don't you go talking to him. If you talk to him, you will get fired quick. He is crazy man." Then Paul knew that the old man did not have a good job at all. He had the worst job in the whole factory. But he didn't know it. He was an ignorant old man, and he believed what you told him.

Maybe the old dipper wasn't crazy at all. Maybe Murphy just said that so nobody would go near him. If people told the old man that it was a bad job, he would get sorry about it, and maybe he would quit. And then you couldn't get anybody else to work there. Paul was sure that he had worked it all out. He was proud of himself for being such a good thinker.

He began to get mad. He figured out what he was going to do about it. Walking back and forth in his room, he saw himself going in to work. First he would go to the piston department and get two pistons. He would put his fists down inside of the pistons and double them up. Then he would go upstairs to the steering-gear department where everybody was working, and he would call Murphy out in the center of the floor. The men would stop working to look at him, and he would swing the heavy pistons around and crack the Irishman on the head five or six times. He would get his arms going like a windmill, and nobody could stop him. He would pound Murphy's head until it was all broken in.

Then he would go and get the old man and say to him: "You come with me. I am going to make something out of you. I am going to give you a chance to get ahead."

The book lay open in front of Paul, and he remembered his promise to read it. He knew he would never get ahead unless he read the book. He sat up in his chair and took hold of some pages.

"I will read this book," he said solemnly. "I will read it to-night. But I am not going to let it make me different. I am not going to get soft like a little boy. I am going to pound that Irishman until his head is sore. I am going to have a big fight to-morrow. But to-night I will read this book. I will go over all the words, but I will not get silly about it like a young kid would. I will not be like that fool Smith with pimples on his face, sitting in the back room of the drug store. I will be like Paul Rinelli. I will be hard; very hard."

THE SAND DOCTOR

THE four Great Lakes that surround Michigan's peninsulas have determined much of the region's history and economic development. Early explorers and missionaries paddled canoes across the "inland seas." The 19th century brought the growth of important fishing and boat building industries. Lake Michigan tempers the climate to make fruit growing possible. Unparalleled scenic beauty and recreational attractions draw thousands of tourists to bolster the economy. With these benefits, however, come the disadvantages of shoreline erosion and sudden storms that have sent hundreds of vessels to the bottom.

Arnold Mulder describes such a storm that wrecked a passenger ferry attempting to reach the harbor at Holland. Mulder knew well the region he wrote about. He grew up in Holland and earned his A.B. Degree from Hope College in 1907. After advanced study at the University of Michigan and the University of Chicago, he returned to become editor and publisher of the HOLLAND SENTINEL.

In 1913 Mulder published his first book, THE DOMINIE OF HARLEM, a story about a Dutch pastor in northern Allegan and Ottawa counties. BRAM OF THE FIVE CORNERS (1915) and THE OUTBOARD ROAD (1919) deal with other themes in the life of the strict Calvinist Hollanders who settled in Allegan and Ottawa counties. He set his final Michigan novel THE SAND DOCTOR (1921), in the city of Holland (Finley). Mulder drew the central character in the story, John Wesley Larramore, from Chase Osborn's autobiographical work, THE IRON HUNTER.

Mulder accepted a teaching position at Kalamazoo College in 1929 as a new experience. He enjoyed teaching and the college so well that he stayed on until retirement in 1953. In addition to his four novels and scores of magazine articles, Mulder published AMERICANS FROM HOLLAND in 1947 and THE KALAMAZOO COLLEGE STORY in 1958.

The Sand Doctor

THE beginnings of Dr. Briar Quentin's life were very closely associated—in Briar's mind at least—with the lake and the dunes. Not the beginnings of his physical life: he was nearly twelve years old when he saw the place for the first time. And then it did not impress him particularly—a winding shore-line of sand hills, tree-be-spattered, and the rest just water. And many of the sand hills seemed rather bare to the boy's eyes; they did not have the fascination, for instance, of a woods where all sorts of interesting things, a rabbit or a nest of bumble-bees, might be lurking.

And during the first two years of the family's life in Finley, after moving there from Chicago because Briar's father could do better for himself in the Finley Belting Works, the boy paid scant attention to the environs of the city. In winter, as a matter of course, he fished through the ice on the river for perch, and in summer he mingled with the summer resorters, marveling at their wealth and the splendor of their gay clothes. But of the dunes he was hardly conscious; and the lake—locally known as the "big lake", to distinguish it from the river which was almost a bay— was only a body of water. It had size, but what was size? You could see only so much of it any-way. That portion of the lake that lay out there beyond the horizon could never have anything to do with him, Briar, until he should sail out into it as he often longed to do when he saw Martin Skager's fishing tug Marie setting out from its little dock in the morning; and when he did sail into it, well, time then to fit it into relevancy with himself.

But that which lay beyond was relevant to him was forced upon him after the family had lived in Finley a year or two. Briar was about fourteen or so at the time, and it was in reality the beginning of himself as a personality—in his own thought of himself at least. Before this he was merely the usual small boy, looked upon by his practically adult sister Mildred as a nuisance when she wanted the porch for herself and young John Nash, of whose recently hung-out lawyer's shingle on Front Street she was very proud. But now abruptly Briar was catapulted into life by the wide spaces of the lake that lay beyond the horizon. They taught him, with Nature's usual sardonic grimness in time of turmoil, that the lake was not merely a body of water. Though what lay beyond the sky-line could not be seen, it could display a power and strike a terror in the heart that a lifetime could not obliterate from the memory. The lake was patient and the hills were placid, and even a fourteen-year-old boy could snap his fingers at them. But when he saw them in the day of their power he understood that if it had not been for what lay beyond the range of vision— the wide fields of water in a landless world under an arching sky—there could never have been the display of power and of terror that in a moment of time changed the whole course of his life.

He petitioned to stay at home with Martin Skager when the rest of the family— his father and mother, nineteen-year-old Mildred, and the "baby", aged nine—went to Chicago to attend the funeral of his maternal grandfather. He calculated that the old fisherman could be induced to take him along on the Marie, and there was more adventure in prospect there than even at a funeral, including a trip to Chicago. He and Martin Skager were great friends, The family readily granted his prayer because the trip would be expensive enough as it was without him.

The trip on the Marie on the second day of his stay at the Skager cottage on the dune side of the river was as exciting as he had expected. But it was the excitement of a boy of fourteen; twenty-four hours later he had aged almost to maturity in outlook.

He was to go again the next day, but Martin Skager, cocking his wise old head to one side, looked dubious.

"I expect your ma wouldn't be stuck on it, Briar, what with this breeze blowin'. It's going to be stiff to-morrow."

But Briar pooh-poohed the fisherman's fears. He was on his own and he was ready to take the responsibility.

173

No. 8 - Steamer Holland, G. & M. Line

"Why, look here, Martin Skager," he said with a great show of reasonableness, "how long you been in the fishing business?"

"Twenty-two year, Briar Quentin," Martin imitated his serious reasonableness, with a gleam of merriment in his eyes.

"An' you never got wrecked all that time— didn't you have some stiff breezes all those years? Still, you ain't dead yet!"

Martin Skager slapped his leg.

"By G—— Christmas!" hastily correcting himself in deference to the boy's youth; "you got a head on you what can figger things out!"

His affection for Briar was genuine. It was almost as exciting for the fisherman to have the boy staying with him as it was for Briar to be there. "Makes a man feel kinda—a—fathery!" he thought, curving his grimy thumbs under his suspenders and stretching the elastic; and his old bachelor soul expanded in the glow of the thought. But it was quite a responsibility. Of course, the little breeze on the lake did not look like anything to Briar who, after a single day's experience, felt that he knew all there was to be known about things maritime and that he would be equal to any situation on the water. Martin Skager knew that the boy was certain to be far more self confident than he, Martin Skager, would dare to be. That was characteristic, not only of boys, but also of grown-ups who had had but a slight taste of life on the lake. Later they became less sure of themselves. "Guess I'd be same way if they'd get me into something I don't know nothin' about," he mused philosophically, —"like bein' President or runnin' a circus or something: I'd think myself a hell-snorter after the first day, an' then I'd begin to learn I didn't know enough to sneeze at!"

"'T ain't the breeze so much, Briar," he demurred to the boy's contempt for what the lake could do to him, "but she smells ugly."

"She?"

"Oh, everything— the air, the lake, the wind," the fisherman explained. "And do you see that?" pointing to a little cloud of dune sand that was caught in a spiral of whirlwind.

"Rats, Martin, what's a little sand?"

Martin Skager smiled.

"*Little!*" verbally underscoring the word; "there's three hundred million tons of it in them dunes—more or less!" he added, in the interest of exact truth.

"But what's sand?"

"What's sand? What's sand?" with curious excitement. "It's—it's—" He struggled for a sufficiently vigorous metaphor. "It's hell, if it has a mind to be," he said at last—"beggin' your pardon, Briar. But it's just that when it takes it into its head. It works slow, but sure as— as— Fate, as a college perfessor would say. Don't you go despisin' no sand, 'specially not dune sand."

The boy was surprised at his friend's earnestness. Martin Skager talked almost as if sand might be dangerous. Sand! He smiled skeptically to himself. Martin Skager in his wisdom understood that smile.

"D' you see them hills out there?" pointing to a group of dunes by themselves that looked like the gathering of a clan. Briar nodded. "That once was Finley— the only Finley there was. But the hills got it into their noodles to tuck the town under nice an' snug an' warm, an' there it is, twenty to fifty feet below the sand. Took quite a spell for the sand to do it, but what's time to sand?"

Briar was impressed. But he was not reconciled to staying at home the next day.

"I guess it'll let up before to-morrow," he said hopefully.

"Maybe," doubtfully, "But she smells ugly."

All night long the wind howled around the little house of Martin Skager in its natural shelter near the river. It was November and rather cold even for that time of the year. Briar in his large bed slept fitfully. He woke up frequently, and every time he listened with a hopefulness that an older person, better acquainted with the heedlessness of the forces of Nature to man and his concerns, could not have maintained. Each time he guessed that it was not blowing as hard as before; but often, even as the thought was forming, the house would shake as if struck a sudden blow by a mammoth flail in the hands of a cosmic giant, and Briar would exclaim, "Rats!" and go to sleep again.

Once when he woke up, passing his tongue over his

lips,he found them gritty. Whatever it was, it got into his mouth, and his teeth crunched on it.

"Sand!" he thought.

He felt over the covers with his hand in the dark. They too felt curiously gritty. He got up to close the window that, to Martin Skager's amusement, he had left open, as Miss Steadfast, the fat city visiting nurse, had taught him in school to do. His bare feet on the board floor felt the sand.

He looked out. The sky was ink, but there was a swirl in the air. Sand, of course, he thought. In the near-distance the roar of the lake drowned out every other sound. The wind was coming in jerky spurts. It seemed to rest from time to time for a moment, and then it struck with a force that was momentarily terrifying. Briar shuddered and ran back to bed. He drew the covers over his head and drew up his knees almost to his chin. The nest was delightfully warm. He shivered, listening to the wind.

"Guess maybe it won't let up," he sighed. It was a dirty shame. To-morrow the family would be back, and it would have to be to-morrow or never.

In the middle of the night the low, dull moan of the foghorn on the piers began to punctuate the noise of the storm. It sent out a long, low blast in a heavy bass voice and then for a few moments it was silent. Again the low blast and again silence. The intervals were carefully measured. Briar could just count thirteen between blasts, counting one to each beat of his heart. He experimented with it, his hand on his breast inside his nightshirt. The exactness with which it worked fascinated him, and for a little while this new alien noise in the welter of other sounds kept him awake. Also, it frightened him a little. There was an ominous sound about the foghorn. He had often heard it in town, but it had never affected him quite this way before. Here, out in the open, with the dunes on one side, the lake on the other, and the river flowing past, it made him shiver a little. He was beginning to appreciate the force of Martin Skager's phrase, "She smells ugly." He understood now that that was not wholly a physical smell.

The loose window frames kept up a continual clatter, as did the doors. Every board in Martin Skager's house seemed to be loose.

"Wonder how the Marie is getting along?" Briar thought. Of course, here in the river at the dock it was never bad— not like out in the big lake, but—

He fell asleep again, and later woke up when Martin Skager came into the house carrying a lantern. Briar was unreasonably surprised. He had not heard the fisherman go out. Sitting up, he blinked into the dim light.

"Went out to tuck the Marie in a little snugger," Martin Skager explained. Then, recurring to the conversation of the evening, "What say, d' you think she'll let up before morning?"

Briar smiled sheepishly, resigned to giving up the trip on the Marie to the fishing grounds. It was good to be safe and warm here with Martin Skager. He no longer felt contemptuous toward the lake. Before Martin Skager had drawn off his rubber boots Briar was asleep.

Down upon the tin roof with its coat of tar came the clatter of rain. It was driven along before the wind, and large blobs of it pelted against the small window panes. But Briar, resigned now and restless no longer, was not wakened by it.

But later, for no reason, he awoke to a curious sense of disaster. The night was still inky black. The foghorn continued to send out its doleful notes, and the roar of the lake was competing with the howl of the wind. There was rain and sand in the air, and the windows and doors were keeping up their insane clatter.

But there was nothing to be afraid of. He was safe. Since he had to give up the trip on the Marie anyway, he was glad it was so stormy that it was wholly out of the question. The stormier the better now, the wilder and noisier, the better. The more impossible the trip, the less he would be regretting it...

But out on the open lake Captain Flint, of the City of Finley, did not share this wish. The City of Finley was a side-wheeler; for years it had been regarded as one of the safest boats of the Hammond Line. And to-night the fat, jolly-eyed captain was not seriously worried. His vessel had come through worse storms than this; although, good sailor that he was, Captain Flint did not despise the present gale. He would not be sorry to be in the shelter of the river, safe at the dock at Finley. The weather was ugly, to be sure, and a good many of the passengers were pretty uncomfortable, but in an hour or two they would be at ease, the boat tied up to the dock. Bucking the storm the City of Finley had lost time, but she would run in between the piers not so very late after all. By daylight the gangplank would be out. The captain looked at his watch calculatingly.

But the next hour brought a surprise even to the experienced Captain Flint. The gale did not progress with a logical increment of force as he had had a reasonable right to expect. Three quarters of an hour out of the harbor there was a tremendous onrush that made the passengers turn white. Not a soul on board, aside from members of the crew off duty, was asleep. People sat on the edge of their berths, eyeing life-preservers; some even were fully dressed. They were ashamed to leave their rooms, but the sound of the gong was not going to catch them unprepared.

"Hell's broke loose right," thought Captain Flint, and it was not as much comfort to him as it was to the passengers that they were near port. The gleam of the intermittent harbor-light at the Finley piers could be seen now and again, and the dull, insistent moan of the foghorn penetrated through the shriller noises of the storm.

Captain Flint had half a mind to ride out the storm in the open lake. The ship could stand it easily. He knew what the City of Finley could do. But the passengers had to be reckoned with. Suppose the blow continued, how would the people take it? He knew from long experience that landlubbers always felt safest hugging the shore; they didn't have the sailor's instinct to stay as far away from the shore as possible in a lake gale. And passengers were a panicky bunch sometimes. To them the open lake looked more ugly than it really was.

He decided to wait for dawn and then make a run for the piers. With some extra precautions the trick could be turned....

He was standing on the bridge, exposed to the pelting of the cold rain, when the nose of the boat, an hour later, was being headed for its dash into the channel. His usually jolly face showed lines of strain. Such passengers as had come out to watch were easy in mind now. They were near something solid, that was all they thought of. But Captain Flint knew that the real test was just beginning. More than one Hammond boat had been swept past the ends of the two long piers at this critical moment and sucked out upon the sandbars beyond to be pounded to pieces during the days that followed— passengers saved, but ship lost.

It was extremely difficult to aim for the middle of the channel in such a sea. Daylight had not yet come, and in the murky indistinctness of things the piers seemed to waver like the ship. Seas were washing over the elevated walk to the lighthouse.

For a moment he had an illusion of having his ship safe, her nose in the exact middle of the channel. It was a difficult feat in a blow like this, and the sailor in him exulted at the technical skill of it. It was beautiful, it was immense. The exact center. Couldn't have been done more neatly on a summer morning in June with nothing bigger than a ripple on the surface of the lake.

Captain Flint's face relaxed its look of strain....

A crash and a bedlam of screams. Then all the lights on the boat went out, leaving the vessel ghastly in the murk of the early dawn.

Captain Flint had no time for surprise. The City of Finley was impaled on the end of the north pier. The lake had had a sardonic surprise for her. Waiting till the very last moment, when the ship's nose was all but in the comparative safety of the channel, a wave picked up the large steel vessel, lifted it bodily out of its course, and deposited it with a crash of cracking steel and splintering wood on the end of the breakwater. It was a display of sheer power that even experienced lake men were not prepared for.

The lights were out, the power shut off, wires broken. Confusion. People swarming to the deck. The vessel hanging precariously on the end of the pier, as if speared by the long arm and held suspended, partly in the water. The deck sloped at a dizzy angle.

There were cries and orders. No one heard anything. But the instinct for life asserted itself. Here below the lower edge of the ship was something solid. It could be seen indistinct in the dawn. People jumped. Helter-skelter. No band playing "Nearer, My God, to Thee." A wild scramble. People picked themselves up as they fell, unheedful of perhaps a broken arm or a sprained ankle. They scurried along the long, wave-swept pier. It was at least solid. Now and again a sea caught a whole group and swept them into the lake, where they disappeared into the gloom of the water.

Eight minutes later the City of Finley fell off its precarious perch. Some people, lost in the confusing blackness when the lights went out, had not had time to reach the deck. Their bodies, some of them, were recovered weeks later....

Briar was at the beach with Martin Skager when the refugees came streaming from the piers. It was not unpleasurable, the wild excitement, and he did not know then that nineteen men and women and children had died within the past ten minutes within a stone's throw of where he stood. Nobody knew until later, though some guessed it.

And neither did he know until some hours later that among the dead were his father, his mother, and his young brother, the "baby." At noon he saw their bodies lying blue and stark in the row on the beach where the lifesaving crew had placed them. Mildred alone of the family had escaped. Some one — a stranger — had told her where to jump and she had obeyed blindly.

Illustration Credits

Page 13—Legends of Michigan and the Old Northwest (1875)

Page 39—Queen of the Woods (1899)

Page 64—100 Years Progress of the U.S. (1871)

Page 76—The Puddleford Papers (1854)

Page 82—Bark Covered House (1876)

Page 100—The Red Kegger (1903)

Page 111—100 Years Progress of the U.S. (1871)

Page 112—100 Years Progress of the U.S. (1871)

Page 120—History of the Great Fires (1871)

Page 141—Report on the Geology and Topography of the Lake Superior Land District (1850)

Page 166—State Archives

Page 174—State Archives